D0935923

# NETWORKING FOR BLACK PROFESSIONALS

## Nonstop Business Networking That Will Change Your Life

N. Renee Thompson, Ph.D.
Michael Lawrence Faulkner, Ph.D.
Andrea R. Nierenberg

ST. JOHN THE BAPTIST PARISH LIBRARY
2920 NEW HIGHWAY 51
LAPLACE, LOUISIANA 70068

Vice President, Publisher: Tim Moore
Associate Publisher and Director of Marketing: Amy Neidlinger
Development Editor: Russ Hall
Operations Specialist: Jodi Kemper
Cover Designer: Chuti Prasertsith
Managing Editor: Kristy Hart
Project Editor: Katiè Matejka
Copy Editor: Krista Hansing, Editorial Services
Proofreader: Sara Schumacher
Indexer: Lisa Stumpf
Compositor: Nonie Ratcliff
Manufacturing Buyer: Dan Uhrig

© 2014 by Pearson Education, Inc.
Publishing as Pearson
Upper Saddle River, New Jersey 07458

Pearson offers excellent discounts on this book when ordered in quantity for bulk purchases or special sales. For more information, please contact U.S. Corporate and Government Sales, 1-800-382-3419, corpsales@pearsontechgroup.com. For sales outside the U.S., please contact International Sales at international@pearsoned.com.

Company and product names mentioned herein are the trademarks or registered trademarks of their respective owners.

All rights reserved. No part of this book may be reproduced, in any form or by any means, without permission in writing from the publisher.

Printed in the United States of America

First Printing December 2013

ISBN-10: 0-13-376012-X
ISBN-13: 978-0-13-376012-5

Pearson Education LTD.
Pearson Education Australia PTY, Limited.
Pearson Education Singapore, Pte. Ltd.
Pearson Education Asia, Ltd.
Pearson Education Canada, Ltd.
Pearson Educación de Mexico, S.A. de C.V.
Pearson Education—Japan
Pearson Education Malaysia, Pte. Ltd.
Library of Congress Control Number: 2013950155

*To all the professionals of color who have made networking
a tool of their success and continued success.*

# Table of Contents

# Foreword

When I retired from professional baseball, I was asked to join the car business by one of the owners of a baseball team. I had no aspiration of owning a car dealership; however, Ron Tonkin, one of the largest auto dealer group owners in the nation and part owner of the Portland Beavers baseball team, thought I would be good at selling cars. You never know who's looking at your skills or recognizing your potential. Follow destiny, it will take you somewhere. I was in the right place at the right time and connected to the right person—a simple definition for *networking*.

During that time, a lot of pressure was being placed upon the automobile industry for minorities to run or be partners in dealerships. I knew that I had to bring more to the table than just being a minority. I had the 3 C's (**C**ompetitive edge, **C**ompetence, and **C**onfidence) to make this opportunity a reality. I was under a lot of pressure and assumed full responsibility because if I failed as one of the first minority dealers in the country then those behind me wouldn't have a chance. I took my work very seriously, and I knew I would do my best to achieve a successful business of my own.

So when I go to work every day now, I realize this is my business and know what I must do to sustain it. I network with people daily to make quality customer service a priority. I take pride in knowing that my customers are happy. How do I accomplish this? I network. I go out and talk to my customers; I listen and establish practices that produce high customer satisfaction ratings.

Networking and connections are interchangeable terms. Connections are the influencers who can help you get better networked into your targeted industry, or who may even be able to share ideas with you to think about areas to explore that you haven't considered, and connect you to people who you may not otherwise have the opportunity to meet. Meeting the coauthor of this book, Dr. Renee Thompson, is a demonstration of how networking really works. She was introduced to me through someone I met at a conference where I was the guest speaker.

By the way, conferences are great opportunities to network. This is the perfect place to walk up to someone and introduce yourself, exchange business cards, place a note on the back of your business card, and of course, compliment the speaker.

Dr. Renee actually employed her networking strategies by reaching out to me directly. I was not a member of her strong ties (people in your immediate circle) as referenced in this book; I was a weak tie (people who are not in your close-knit group, a population or audience that would not be accessible). Apparently, there is strength in weak ties so be sure to take advantage of what is offered in this book for African American professionals. This book provides a step-by-step guide, as well as strategies and tips on how to expand your networking opportunities by going beyond your immediate circle. Don't let fear hold you back, take the ride and see where it leads you!

Dorian Boyland,
President of Boyland Auto Group.
*(4th largest African-American dealership in the United States.)*

# Acknowledgments

Thank you to Tim Moore, Publisher of Pearson Education for his hands-on ability to make things happen and for his superior skills that have made many books like this very successful. A huge thank you to all of the people at Pearson who contributed their amazing skills in pulling this book together. Thank you to Russ Hall for his gift in writing and extraordinary editorial talents.

We are also so thankful to Frank Burrows of Pearson Learning Solutions for his belief in us and for introducing us to Sean Stowers, also of Pearson Learning Solutions, who thinks out of the box and was the one who networked us into the organization and opened the door. And thank you to Linda Schuler for her administrative savvy and skills.

Thanks so much to all of you.

# About the Authors

**Dr. N. Renee Thompson** is the founder and president of a non-profit organization, Transitions Education Center (TEC), and employed as an associate dean of the College of Liberal Arts & Sciences at DeVry University. TEC is an organization with a strong foundation that seeks to stimulate and expand educational and sociocultural opportunities for minority and low-income students seeking higher education. Thompson is committed to diversifying the spectrum of college graduates by empowering students to develop professional and leadership skills. She is also the founder of Girlfriends Listen!—a fun-loving core group of women that shares interesting and valuable insight. This group was started to share experiences with other women to empower others to reach their full potential.

**Dr. Michael Lawrence Faulkner** is a U.S. Marine Corps Vietnam veteran who served from 1964 to 1970 and rose to the rank of Staff Sergeant. He spent 30 years in a variety of leadership and management ("coaching") positions with Dun & Bradstreet, the Direct Marketing Association (DMA), and entrepreneurial start-ups, as well as helping run the family business before moving into the academic world. Today Michael is a professor at the Keller Graduate School of Management at DeVry University. Michael is a member of MENSA, a former two-time national champion of Athletic Dueling, and an International Rotary Fellowship award winner. He has been published in peer review journals, dozens of magazines, newsletters, websites, and blogs, and has written half a dozen white papers, including one that was circulated to all elected members of Congress and the major media outlets. He has written or coauthored 11 books.

**Andrea R. Nierenberg**, best-selling author, speaker, and world-renowned business authority, is the force behind The Nierenberg Consulting Group. Called a "networking success story" by the *Wall Street Journal*, Andrea founded The Nierenberg Consulting Group in 1993. With a stellar 29 years as a leader in sales and marketing, Andrea is an in-demand business expert both at home and abroad. Her company partners with an array of the world's leading financial and media industry businesses.

# What You Will Learn from This Book

We live in a highly competitive world. Today it is never too early to learn the business and life skills that will give you the competitive edge when you embark upon the networking journey. This book gives you the hands-on steps and processes to take you from your current position (even if you're a student or unemployed) to a job, a promotion, and subsequent leadership positions. *You will learn that you might already be networking—you just might not call it that.* You will learn everything from creating connections to being aware of how each person you meet can be a potential connection who you can help—and who could possibly help you.

# 1

# What Is Networking, and Is It Any Different for African Americans Than Anyone Else?

Individually, you are unique and special—just as everyone else is. And everyone has the same choice to makex, at about the same time, about whether and how to network. Unfortunately, and this is where you begin to separate yourself, the vast majority of people won't recognize the moment of networking opportunity and, therefore, won't have the same choices that you will. What separates you from them is that you are reading this book and opening your mind to the networking possibilities that await you.

This missed opportunity is so unfortunate for all the others because this is a choice of whether you will have maximum control over your own pathways to life's success via networking. This is one of the few egalitarian moments in life when you have the opportunity to experience near-perfect *equality of opportunity for your own future.* This is a moment when you decide on the equality of the outcome of your choices.

## WHAT'S BEHIND YOUR CONCEPT OF SELF

Psychologists call the belief of self-empathy "internal locus of control." Skeptics and doubters, whom Michael refers to as sheep-like people, are those who prefer to live their lives among flocks of others like themselves, who dress alike, look alike, talk alike, work alike, think alike, act alike, believe alike, and like alike. They want you to believe that life has a kind of predestined pathway. These people believe that life is like a linear path—certain things are expected of you at certain times, and certain things either come your way or don't. In other words, you have no control over life.

Psychologists sometimes talk about the self-concept theory (SCT), which simply states that many of the successes and failures people experience in their careers and lives are closely tied to the ways they are accustomed to viewing themselves through their relationships with other people, including their parents, teachers, spouses, partners, bosses, managers, and supervisors.

SCT brings up three critical points. First, self-concept is learned; we're not born with it. We learn it through repeated experiences, and it's rooted in our expected outcomes of those experiences, particularly experiences with people in more powerful or influential roles. Second, self-concept is organized. We organize the feelings, beliefs, and worldview of our self-concept because we generally desire order and harmony in our lives. Lastly, self-concept is dynamic, meaning that we view the world not in isolation, but in relation to our self-concept, which is subject to continuous reevaluation as we attempt to assimilate new ideas and get rid of old ones. Individuals try to maintain their self-concepts regardless of how helpful or damaging to themselves or others these self-concepts become. This truth is evidenced by individuals who often sacrifice physical and financial comfort and even their own safety to achieve emotional satisfaction and avoid change.

Individuals experience anxiety because of a loss of self-esteem, and anything that negatively impacts self-concept risks depleting self-esteem. You can make SCT work for you or allow it to work against you. Most importantly, SCT is within each individual's control. Some people accept this; some people reject it. If you accept it, you exercise internal locus of control and are ready to make the choices to control your own life.

Some people (not necessarily just the sheep) believe life is full of unexpected randomness and troubles that will continually pop up, negating any preparations or plans we make. These people believe the best we can do is manage these problems and obstacles and live with those outcomes.

By this point in your life, you have probably dealt with a wide range of issues—and you might still be struggling with them, perhaps overcoming obstacles and problems with school and work; dealing with your fears, loneliness, and career aspirations; coping with concerns about job search issues; worrying about how to meet people; managing your fear of public speaking, making new friends, and joining groups; and navigating many, many other life issues.

You don't have to face most of these issues and problems alone. In fact, you *shouldn't* face them alone. Superman, Batman, and plenty of other superheroes had sidekicks to help them—what makes any one of us think we can handle life alone? *Don't be afraid or egotistical enough to think that you don't need the help of other people.* You do. Only a fool believes he or she can succeed alone.

The thing is, you might not currently know the people who can best help you, or hire you, or move you forward. You need to reach out to them. That's where networking comes in. Networking is the most successful technique and tool used by the most successful individuals in all walks of life, regardless of gender, religion, industry or profession, level of intelligence and education, age, social situation, and geographic area. This isn't the tool of a secret society. Just about everybody has the opportunity to learn the techniques and tools of networking for success. Whether you reach out and grasp this opportunity is up to you. But—and this is the important thing—you have as good an opportunity as anyone!

## Defining Networking

Does the word *networking* scare you or make you cringe? Are you fearful of what it might imply? Does the word imply that you have to meet strange or different people, or introduce yourself to people who might reject you? Or do you feel that networking is just some form of glad-handing or "sucking up," and that people who network get ahead because of *who* they know, not *what* they know? And even if the myth "It's who you know, not what you know, that counts" were true, why would you ignore this pathway to success? Do you believe there's something inherently sinister, bad, or unfair about using contacts to help you get ahead?

Networking pioneer and guru George Fraser is known as the "King of Networking." He proposed effective networking to the black community in 1994 in his book *Success Runs in Our Race.* Fraser defined effective networking as follows: "[E]ffective networking is the identification, building and developing of relationships for the purposes of sharing information and resources." Fraser said that networking is consistent with garnering information and equated it with a source of power: "[A]ny information flows to anyone willing to receive it. It is not racist, or elitist, or exclusive. That is what makes networking so effective."

*Networking* is one of the most overused and misunderstood words in common vocabulary today. When you hear the word, what comes to your mind?

- Getting something from someone else
- Using others
- Coercion
- Manipulation
- Getting something without using your real abilities
- Having a "godfather" or mentor who will smooth the way for you even if you're not capable or qualified
- Making hundreds of daily short digital contacts on social network sites

Or, do the following descriptions come to mind?

- Enrichment
- Empowerment
- The chance to learn something new
- The opportunity to meet interesting people
- The best method to achieve a professional or personal goal
- The real world—the way most jobs are filled, far more than any other method of job searching

Perhaps you've heard the statistics and seen the evidence, or you've seen your friends' networking turn into opportunity after opportunity for them. Maybe you'd like to network but feel that your chances of networking aren't as great as others' because you're a black person, or maybe you feel that you don't have the experience, skills, or abilities to network properly.

You might even play host to one of those ornery critters who appears every once in a while to sit on your shoulder (invisible, of course, to everyone but you) and criticize you unmercifully, trying to convince you of how unworthy you are because you're a black person. That character will try to dissuade you from ever trying to network because you're not worthy. Now is the perfect time to put your fears and uneasiness to rest, bury your concerns, change your beliefs, and ban that critter—that is, if you really want the greatest opportunities for success in life.

If you want the greatest chances for success in getting the jobs you desire and deserve; meeting the people who are ready and willing to assist you in your aspirations; being considered for the career opportunities you dream about; positioning yourself for the best promotions; being asked to serve on exciting committees; and working with the most prestigious, influential, important people in the fields, industries, professions, and communities of *your* choice—if you want to have control of these choices, then it's in your hands. It's your choice.

As a black individual, you might have faced—and continue to face—many challenges on a daily basis that are not overtly racial. You might feel sure that many silent or behind-the-scenes obstacles prevent you from obtaining certain positions or committee spots.

However, you will learn that networking is a crucial component in career advancement. First, you need to learn the networking game and its rules via observation. It pays to watch the players before entering the game. While watching, develop yourself professionally by obtaining the necessary skill set, certifications, and degrees to be a competitor on the team. No one wants a handout—being qualified gets you in the game. Second, after watching the game, you need exposure. Seek out the invitation to play in the game by attending meetings, seminars, workshops, and work-related functions—after all, you can't get in the game if you're not attending opportunities for networking. Lastly, begin building relationships, and perhaps seek out a mentor to help you navigate the process.

Of course, if you don't want any of these opportunities, or if you think that getting them by having people help you would somehow diminish your character, then stop here. Other people will gladly take the help of those who are willing to assist. A great deal of research proves something you probably know intuitively: Networking works for those who choose to work networking.

By an enormous margin, networking is the single most effective technique for finding jobs (even during economic recessions), building a career, developing personal influence, solidifying leadership roles, strengthening effective management skills, developing personal communication skills, creating and improving organizational skills, learning how to work with individuals with diverse views, developing beliefs and skills, and generally enhancing the quality of your life. Thousands of individuals of every race, culture, and diversity segment can attest to this.

The talent to network is inherent in nearly every individual. Almost anyone can learn how to network. However, only those who have the drive, energy, skills, and knowledge to learn and perfect the network process will be able to use it to their advantage.

Therefore, although most people instinctively know—or can eventually figure out—that networking "works" (which is why we get the myth that it's who you know that counts), only a limited number of devoted individuals manage to reap the huge rewards of successful networking. A study of UCLA graduates found that nearly 75 percent believed it was who you knew that counted. What's interesting about this finding is that three-quarters of the graduates believed they knew the secret to success, yet they couldn't bring themselves to actually do what it took and become networkers.

The U.S. Department of Labor reports that 80 percent of all the newly created jobs in the last decade were never posted or announced anywhere. Furthermore, 70 percent of the replacement jobs were handled in the same manner. These jobs weren't posted on any website, advertised on any classified page, listed with any headhunter or recruiter, or otherwise publicly posted. These jobs were filled by the hiring managers' use of their social networking. The hiring managers first looked at people they knew and trusted, and if that didn't turn up the candidate they wanted, they asked their network—their own contacts, *the people they knew and trusted.* Current research by Professors Michael Faulkner and Bruce Herniter at DeVry University on the impact of networking has found that personal networking and focused, direct contact with the hiring manager account for more job hunting success by job seekers than all the other methods combined.

The important issue is simply that the overwhelming number of jobs in America are filled through the process of networking. If you don't use networking skills, you surrender many job, life, and other opportunities to other people. You deserve the benefits of networking, but you have to reach out and take them.

People already in the workforce who have learned to take advantage of the skills and benefits of networking will confirm that they get many more opportunities than their peers who do not network. Unfortunately, many African Americans aren't aware of the value of networking and thus don't practice the skills; consequently, they can't take advantage of the benefits, leaving this enormous opportunity untapped.

In just one area, jobs, networking can mean the difference between jump-starting your career and spending years working unsatisfying, unfulfilling dead-end jobs. In April 2011, the U.S. Department of Labor reported that the national unemployment rate was 9 percent—and the unemployment rate for African Americans was 16.1 percent (versus 8 percent for whites). Some evidence by economists indicates that unemployment will be a societal problem in America for years into the future. Networking could mean the difference between being part of the pool of African Americans working in low-level, unsatisfying jobs and moving your career along regardless of the state of economy.

Knowing how the hiring process really works is just half of the benefit of networking. The other half is knowing in advance what hiring managers really want in new hires. In a number of empirical research studies conducted over the past ten years, senior managers of a wide range of businesses were asked about what they were looking for in candidates. The following is what they said they value most, starting with the most frequently cited skills, characteristics, and talents:

- Good communication skills
- Interpersonal skills
- Ability to find and fix problems
- Enthusiasm

- High energy level

- Strength of character

- Self-confidence

- Motivation

- Leadership skills

- Quick adaptability to change and uncertainty

- Good listening skills

- Commitment to lifetime learning

- Commitment to excellence

- Ability to work as a team player

- Willingness to take some risks

- Willingness to face self-assessment

- Ability to lighten up (to not take oneself too seriously)

In a nationwide study conducted in 1999 by a well-known executive search consulting firm, 27 percent of chief information officers reported that strong interpersonal skills were the single most important quality in job candidates (23 percent listed this as the second-most-important skill).[1]

A major research study conducted for an association of colleges and universities found that a significant majority of respondents cited skills learned and perfected in networking as the most important skills employers look for in new hires. Specifically, those skills are teamwork (44 percent), critical thinking (33 percent), and oral/written communications (30 percent).

In a poll conducted in June 2009, Michael asked business managers and supervisors about the most important skills and traits for recent college graduates. A total of 293 respondents provided the answers in Table 1-1.

**Table 1-1**

| Skill/Trait | Percent of Respondents |
|---|---|
| Potential to learn or be trained | 40% |
| Interpersonal/team skills | 23% |
| Communication skills | 13% |
| Proven achievement/experience | 12% |
| Technical/technology knowledge | 9% |

Michael Faulkner–LinkedIn, 2009

This poll reaffirms employers' high regard for the soft skills and talents—the ability to learn, the ability to get along, and communication skills.

So if the idea of networking scares you or puts you off, or if for some reason you think that networking isn't for you because you're black, there's something important for you to know:

- First, you're not alone. Believing you're on your own might be a reason you've shied away from the very skill that can help you professionally and personally.

- Second, you don't have to wait and try to learn the benefits of networking as you mature or advance in your career. The earlier you overcome the fear or obstacle that hinders you, the sooner you will start gaining the benefits of networking. This is the skill that can begin helping you.

Let's deal with the negative and inaccurate impressions of networking right now. In some of the negative impressions we listed, some people express a dark side of networking. It really isn't even networking they're discussing—it's the dark side of human characteristics. Some individuals abuse networking, so it can be easy to confuse that abuse with networking itself. We've said that networking is the most powerful tool individuals can use in their careers and lives. It shouldn't come as any surprise, then, that some people out there aren't benevolent, gracious, nice, friendly, kind, fair, and helpful individuals. Sure, you'll find the occasional malevolent, malicious, spiteful, wicked, nasty, mean, power-hungry, self-centered, egotistical, narcissistic jerk. These bad seeds can just as easily master the understanding of body language and fake networking techniques to fool some people for a short period of time; those rotten apples can use their genes, money, power (not influence), and even evil to get ahead.

Other people advance solely on the coattails of a godfather or mentor. But they're quickly seen as empty suits and frequently are abandoned or exiled. They eventually fail or wither away in ignominious insignificance. All these examples show how networking gets an inaccurate and even bad name. But these people aren't networking—they're power brokering and using power tactics instead of influence.

## Why Networking Works: You Already Have the Resources You Need—You Just Have to Put Them to Work

Scientist John Milgram developed a theory called the small world theory that suggests that everyone in the world is separated from everyone else by just six contacts. Dr. Milgram did a series of famous experiments that proved his theory. More recently, Dr. Nicholas Christakis and Dr. James Fowler wrote a book called *Connections*, in which they thoroughly investigate the small world theory and others on human social connections. They reaffirm the important influence a person's network can have on job searching. If you use the social Internet site LinkedIn, you can see how the six degrees connection is possible by the raw numbers of third-level contacts or what Christakis and Fowler call "friends of friends." For example, in 2010, Michael had 183 LinkedIn contacts. These 183 contacts give him the potential to reach all those contacts' individual network contacts, and all of those contacts/friends give him the opportunity to reach all *their* network contacts (friends, friends of friends). That totals more than 2,530,000 third-level contacts, more than anyone could ever contact in a lifetime. The implication for networking is profound, even if you were to actively network with only a tiny fraction of the potential you're capable of reaching. Each network contact you have is likely already networked, which, given the proper approach, care, and feeding, means your contacts should grow by some multiple.

The key phrase here is "proper approach, care, and feeding." Your network is available for you to enrich your professional and personal life, but in return, you must enrich the lives of others.

Michael and Andrea get very upset when they hear someone say, "It's time to start looking for a job. I'd better start networking." Or they might say, "I only network at certain meetings or events." Unfortunately, a great deal of the research shows that most of the success from networking comes to white workers who are 24 years of age or older and moving into their second or third job. This doesn't mean this is the only group that can successfully network; it simply means that, up to this point, it's the only sample group researchers have chosen to examine.

Networking is a skill—and like any personal skill, it needs to be practiced to be perfected. You can't just sit down at a piano once a month and play Bach concertos like they are supposed to be played—nor can you network properly on demand whenever the need might arise. Networking is a five-step process that's simple to define but involves hard work:

> **Step 1: Meet people.** Some people you know; some you don't at first. You have to mix it up and get to know them. In Chapter 4, "Creating Connections: The People You Will Need in Your Network," we introduce examples of "breaking the ice" phrases that you can use or adapt to your own style.

> **Step 2: Listen and learn.** All people like to talk about themselves and/or their company. When you actively listen, you learn about what's important to other people, who they are, how you could help them, and how they could help you. In Chapter 5, "Characteristics of Great Networkers," we discuss the difference between real empathetic listening (when you engage in active and responsive listening) and listening in which you're just "hearing" what someone said.

> **Step 3: Make connections.** Help people connect with others you know can help them. When you help your contacts get what they want, you can't help but be successful yourself.

**Step 4: Follow up.** Keep your promises; keep your word. If you promise to do something, do it in a timely manner. In Chapter 8, "Keeping Your Network Alive and Growing," we show you an easy-to-use method for following up with contacts.

**Step 5: Stay in touch.** After an initial period of contact, if a result doesn't materialize, most people just move on. Here's where your own networking system will make you successful. These folks find ways to stay in touch and continue to build relationships. Why? Because their goal is to build a network of long-lasting, mutually beneficial relationships, not just to get an immediate "result."

This five-step system works because it's based on building long-lasting relationships—not just immediate relationships, but lifelong ones.

Networking is lifelong and beneficial to everyone who participates. It's a win–win proposition. On the other hand, power brokering, by its nature, is a zero-sum political contest in which someone must win and someone must lose. In the long run, an individual who practices power brokering creates a long list of enemies who will do anything they can to bring down that person. Unlike net workers, power brokers have few friends. Real net workers gain the positive benefits listed earlier because they gain the help and assistance of an ever-growing number of people.

# Endnote

1. Clifford Gray and Erik Larson, *Project Management: The Managerial Process,* 4th ed. (New York: McGraw-Hill Irwin, 2008).

# 2

# How to Network Effectively

**N**o one can forecast success for every endeavor, but if you learned there's a success rate of better than 60 percent for engaging in a particular behavior, wouldn't you want to learn as much about that behavior as possible? Well, prepare to alter your behavior—and probably your beliefs.

According to research conducted by Cornell University Career Services, 85 percent of the newly created jobs in America and 75 percent of the jobs for replacement positions are never posted anywhere. This means these jobs are never listed on the Internet; recruiters and headhunters don't know about them; postings don't appear on Craigslist, MySpace, or Monster.com; and the respective human resources departments might not even be aware of them in advance. The only people who know about the open positions are the hiring managers and their networks.

One of the fundamental credos of both networking and human nature is that people are nesters and prefer to be around and work with other people they know and like. This is not a mystery of the universe or a great discovery of science; it's simply human nature.

Given the opportunity, hiring managers first attempt to hire people they know and like. This makes sense. A manager will spend eight to ten hours a day with an employee during a normal work day, not to mention any additional hours traveling or engaging in social activities. The manager wants to hire someone he or she will enjoy spending time with. In addition, the manager wants to be certain that the employee is trustworthy—and trust and reciprocity are traits and talents that can't be taught.

Managers can teach new employees the job requirements; they can't teach new employees to get along with others, unilaterally find and fix problems, have good interpersonal skills, be adaptable to change or uncertainty, or be willing to take risks. These kinds of traits and talents typically define people managers find from their own networks. If hiring managers can't find someone they know and like, they extend their personal network of contacts and ask others they know and like for referrals of anyone they know who could fill the position. People put great stock and trust in their contacts' networks. If a contact knows and likes someone, that candidate has (unbeknown to them) already made a great first impression on the hiring manager.

If hiring managers can't find candidates they know, or candidates a network contact knows, only then do they put the traditional job-hunting approaches and tools to work searching for qualified prospects. Finally, if no one with experience turns up, managers interview prospects with "potential," usually the code word for a recent college graduate or a college student about to graduate. Even if the word *networking* makes you cringe, you should at least be aware that you need to develop this skill to be successful. Don't buy into the myth that there's something wrong with the expression, "It's not what you know, but who you know." This old saying is truer than ever in today's competitive world.

Most often, the "who you know" does *not* necessarily lead you to the next job, the next new client, the funding for your new business, the successful new project in your company, or whatever you're looking for in life professionally or personally. Rather, it leads to the *opportunity* to be in the position to be considered for the job, meet the potential new client, gain a favorable introduction and positive meeting with funders, enjoy favorable consideration for a new project, or garner any number of professional or personal opportunities that others will not get.

Networking isn't a tool by which you should expect to be handed gifts that you're not qualified for or given responsibilities you're not capable of handling. For example, you and your boss might discuss the proverbial question, "Where do you see yourself in this company in a few years?" If you're talking about a specific position that appeals to you, the more significant question might be, "Can you handle the job?"

Networking and expressing your interests in positions are only half the feat; the other half is based on your competence.

"Who you know" is hardly ever enough in itself to get someone anything (unless you have the same last name and DNA of the other person). What you want from networking is the inside track, the most favored treatment, the full and undivided attention of the decision maker or influencer to make your case. This, of course, is something the other candidates almost never get.

Extensive research has delved into what employers look for in new hires, and firms repeatedly name four traits: (1) skills, (2) knowledge, (3) experience, and (4) talents. The skills managers want are the soft skills we've already mentioned, such as communication skills, interpersonal skills, the ability to find and fix problems, and a work ethic. Networking experiences develop and reinforce these skills. The knowledge component consists of a job applicant's intelligence.

The experience issue isn't a critical matter if the hiring manager is already sold on your intelligence and skill level. An intelligent applicant can be taught most jobs. The real issue is talent. Most firms aren't good at assessing an individual's talents, an applicant's recurring patterns of thought, feelings, actions, and behaviors that naturally equip the individual to excel in a job. Therefore your use of networking and communication skills allows you to take charge, to demonstrate your talents and how you will benefit the employer.

What do you as an applicant have to do?

- Demonstrate how you will reduce the cost of the hire, lower the employee turnover rate, and improve interpersonal relationships with other employees.

- Demonstrate that you are easy to manage, can quickly learn roles, can adapt quickly to change, and, therefore, have a shorter learning curve.

- Demonstrate that you will be more productive, more precise, and more consistent; will miss less work; will produce higher-quality work; will make fewer mistakes; will reduce management anxiety and stress; and will exceed expectations.

- Demonstrate that you will produce greater customer satisfaction, greater customer retention, and higher profits.

To do all this, you need time and the undivided attention of the decision maker. You need the decision maker to start with a favorable opinion of you and allow you to build your case from there.

Andrea's photographer friend, Judy, knows all this. This well-educated, competent, professional woman has many contacts from her previous career as a marketing manager and knows the value of marketing herself. Judy knows she has to overcome her resistance to networking, yet she can come up with a million and one excuses not to network.

Renee is a psychologist, founder of two organizations, and past dean at DeVry University. To reach people to participate in her organizations, she needed to network. She used all her contacts to promote her organizations. She hand-selected board members who would be effective and whose background and experience would benefit the organization. Most of her contacts are close friends she developed through work relationships, church, and friends' recommendations, who in turn, use their contacts when promoting Renee's organizations. She established a tree of networking that has blossomed into other contacts that have partnered with her organizations.

Michael is a professor at DeVry University. In his career-development course, Michael spends a lot of time focusing on networking. He has his students make a list of 25 people they know by first name. From this list, the students pick a half dozen contacts and then make calls from the classroom, write letters, and seek to set up networking meetings with two to three contacts. In this step-by-step approach, Michael attempts to show the students that networking isn't something to be feared and that everyone can it do with a little effort.

The experiences of many, including Judy, Renee, and Michael's college students are fairly common. When we ask others to share their reactions to networking, we get the following reactions. Do any sound familiar to you?

- "I'm really a shy person."
- "I wouldn't know where to begin."

- "People judge me by the color of my skin and aren't interested in my experience and skills."

- "No one would be interested in me or what I have to say."

- "I tried making contacts [networking] once. After three months, nothing happened so I gave up."

- "I'm uncomfortable starting a conversation with a stranger."

- "I don't know how to keep a conversation going or how to gracefully break away when it's time to move on."

- "I'm embarrassed and too proud to ask someone for a favor."

- "I'm a private person. When I get on a plane or a train, the last thing I want to do is chat with the person next to me."

- "I'm busy. I hardly have enough time in my life to kiss up to the white man."

- "I don't care for the type of people who call themselves 'networkers.' I think they're only interested in getting something from me."

- "I don't know how to keep track of my contacts. My address book is a mess, and I don't have a PDA or the right software on my computer."

- "I haven't followed through with the contacts I've managed to make; therefore, when I do need more information or help, I'm reluctant to make the call."

- "I'm young. I have plenty of time to network later in my career."

- "I'm black, and black people don't have any opportunities to meet people who count or who are important."

- "With the degree I'm getting, it's such a specialty that I won't need much networking in my field."

- "As a black person, I don't have that much work experience to tell people about. Besides, I'm already viewed as a second-class person."

- "I'm in the [engineering, computer, security, database, nursing, construction, mining, manufacturing, etc.] field. Nobody does networking in my field."

Renee can relate to these feelings, since she's a black woman who deals with the race barrier daily. Networking has become easier for all of us—but it isn't always easy. Andrea and Michael were both very shy. Although Renee wasn't shy, her reluctance in networking stemmed from her perspective of being different, black, and deficient. She didn't think she'd be accepted in "their world" by the majority stakeholders, whites. Networking became less threatening and fearful for Renee as she gained more experience and skills—and, most of all, as she became more educated. She embraced and understood the concept better: If she was qualified, her race might become a secondary obstacle in networking. When she began to feel that she was playing equally (educationally) on the same field as the stakeholders, she became more comfortable with networking. She realized that she "put in" the work not to be "put down" by anyone.

Likewise, you must gain the confidence to enter the networking world, or you won't discover your opportunities. When Andrea first moved to New York City, she knew no one except her grandparents. Today she has a database of more than 2,500 people, and it's still growing. She'll tell you that she found out that networking was the one sure way she could enrich and empower herself early in her career.

Michael grew up painfully shy and self-conscious, using self-deprecating humor and athletics to cover for his low self-esteem. He also has a learning disability, but he didn't discover that until he was an adult and had learned his own successful coping mechanisms through trial and error. Before then, he'd faced many, many failures.

Consider Andrea's basic theory on networking: Networking is the opposite of *not* working. As she says, "In other words, if you're not making connections and nurturing the relationships you have developed, you are simply *not working.*"

# Adopting Effective Attitudes and Behaviors for Networking

To allow networking to work for you, to benefit both your life and your prospects' lives, you need to *prepare to alter your behavior and probably your beliefs.* This statement is quite profound when it comes to networking. What does this statement imply? Do you need to change who you are or change your beliefs to network? Do you need to be a "sellout" to succeed in the workplace? No, the statement merely implies that you might have to learn new behaviors and attitudes and possibly change your beliefs to be successful at networking.

For example, if you believe you're not "good enough" to get the job because you're a black person, you might be unconsciously sending signals to others that indicate the same. You must replace this type of negative belief with a positive one by utilizing a psychological approach that you can practice. But you can't change if you're not aware of your belief and its associated behavior.

Your behavior illustrates your level of confidence. (Learn more about portraying confidence in Chapter 5, "Characteristics of Great Networkers.") You might have to arm yourself with a new attitude, which your behavior will then reflect. Remember, your mind (thought processes) determines your attitude and behavior.

## First Impressions

Psychologists have asserted that people make up their minds about others they meet for the first time because expectations influence visual perception. It's very difficult for people to disbelieve what they see with their own two eyes. Therefore, rejecting a first impression is a complex cognitive task wherein you attempt to deny a first impression. I strongly recommend that you not make the mistake of underestimating the power of the first impression.

Research studies conducted by Princeton professors Willis and Todorvo[1] indicate that it takes a tenth of a second to form an impression of a stranger from his or her facial expression—and longer exposure might not significantly alter those impressions. The professors conducted individual studies examining judgments from facial appearance, each focusing on a different trait: trustworthiness, aggressiveness, competence, attractiveness, and likeability. The results indicated participants made their judgment within the quick time frame of one-tenth of a second. Longer exposure time increased confidence in judgments. In summary, the initial information the brain receives about anything influences how information is processed later. First impressions are easily made and not so easy to undo.

Although you have only one opportunity to give others a sample or slice of who you are to make the first impression, that opportunity represents nearly 100 percent of what they get to know about you in a very short period of time. You want this sample to be an accurate representation of who you are. Suppose you're a baker entering a baking contest. The judge doesn't need to eat the entire pie to make an assessment—a few forkfuls is usually sufficient. There's a presumption that the pie will taste the same regardless of the amount the judge eats. Similarly, you want to prepare your best recipe for success (confidence, competence, politeness, positive body language, and so on). You want the slice of *you* to leave a favorable impression while networking.

In addition, negative behavioral impressions are heavily weighed, especially if your body language appears distracted or self-absorbed. Body language should be relaxed as possible, according to body language expert Linda Talleys.[2] She recommends the following:

1. Make eye contact. Hold the other person's gaze for 2–4 minutes, with a genuine smile (the universal gesture of validation).

2. Use good posture, with your shoulders back. You might have to change your physiology before you change your psychology.

3. Don't be weighed down. Ditch the backpack, briefcase, and handbag—travel small and light.

4. Offer a solid handshake to convey confidence and a willingness to build a relationship.

(See Chapter 5 for more information on nonverbal body language.)

More specifically, consider the historically negative and inaccurate impressions of black people. For example, Michelle Obama appeared on the cover of *Time* magazine with a machine gun in her hand and a stereotypical Afro-centric hairstyle. No matter how black people try to debunk the myths, the stereotypes live on, up to the highest-ranking positions in America. Not even the First Lady, an Ivy League graduate, is exempt.

The Princeton study we mentioned earlier points out two stereotypical traits, attractiveness and likeability, that African Americans silently face when networking. Many research studies have revealed that attractive people not only are hired faster than less attractive people, but also have a higher likeability factor than less attractive people. Taking a closer look, African Americans are viewed less or more attractive based on the different hues of their skin color.

A darker hue translates into less attractive and more aggressive. In contrast, a lighter hue is interpreted as more attractive and less threatening. Why? Basically, the lighter hue is a closer match to the expectancy (visual perception) of society's majority race.

Yet people hire those they trust. Black people aren't always seen as neighbors or trusted others; they could be seen as different and deficient. We all are familiar with the saying, "I have a black friend." What does this mean? "I know one black person I can trust." Looking beyond the stereotypes and statistics, the images and numbers tell only part of the story. Don't let the numbers represent your story. Historically, African-American success stories are based on "firsts"—the first black President, the first black governor, the first black CEO, the first generation educated, and so on. Successful networking attitudes and behaviors are colorblind, though; good manners (behaviors) are good manners, regardless of who demonstrates them. Don't allow stereotypes to hinder your ability to sell yourself when you're networking. Clearly, that doesn't mean you need to "sell out," either.

To clarify, the term "selling out" is often used to describe a black person who is intelligent and educated, speaks well, and is perceived to be acting against the interest of his or her race for the benefit of money. Randall Kennedy, a Harvard law professor, defines a "sellout" when used in a racial context as an African American who knowingly or with gross negligence acts against African Americans as a whole—these sell-outs are seen as dangerously antagonistic to other African Americans' well-being and, ultimately, as traitors to the black race.

There's a strong connection between those perceptions and being an "Oreo," someone who looks black but thinks or acts white. It's unlikely that either of these ideologies will hold true when networking because the perspective is limited to African Americans and probably not recognizable by other races. Oprah Winfrey gave a commencement address at Howard University in May 2007 and told the graduates: "Do not be a slave to any form of selling out." In other words, you don't have to lose your identity and adopt other ethnic behaviors, nor do you have to fake any behavior or attitude to succeed.

However, you do need to understand the rules of the networking game to be successful at networking. Keep in mind the rule of sheep: The flock wants to drag down the pioneers, explorers, leaders, and "sellouts." The flock is secure when everyone is the same—when no single member is excelling or demonstrating personal greatness. If networking is selling out, then get busy selling out and leave them in the dust.

Keith Wyche, the author of *Good Is Not Enough: And Other Unwritten Rules,* pointed out that black people make up approximately 13 percent of the U.S. population, but they fall woefully short in black representation at the top of corporate America. Although black people have made tremendous progress in obtaining top-notch positions in many areas besides sports, there's still room for improvement. Catalyst, a nonprofit research organization, reports that women hold 50.3 percent of top management and professional positions, yet they make up less than 2 percent of the CEOs at Fortune 500 and Fortune 100 publicly traded companies. The dismal numbers are quite perplexing.

Wyche emphasized the importance of knowing the rules before you play the game. For example, he indicated that the banking and finance industry tends to be conservative and formal, whereas high-tech organizations and the media industry tend to be less formal and more liberal in both operations and dress code. Similarly, the utility industry leans toward a historical "entitlement" culture based on seniority and internal promotions, whereas the sales industry tends to promote and reward based on individual performance.

Even after you learn the rules of networking and how to get to the interview stage to obtain the job, you face the ongoing challenge of personal retention. How do you maintain your position and seek growth? At that point, you need to develop an in-house network and persona by learning the company's unwritten code of conduct.

For instance, you can try asking key players in the company whether you should attend the holiday party or the company cookout, inquire about how ideas are expressed and to whom, and learn about other corporate culture issues. When asking questions, be certain to *listen* to what is being said and what is not. Greek philosopher Epictetus said we have two ears and one mouth so that we can listen twice as much as we speak. For example, when you're asking whether you should attend the holiday party, if you receive a nonchalant answer such as "It's up to you," your instincts should tell you to explore the question further or ask another key player to gain more insight about the culture. As Wyche suggests, you need to learn the company's ideology, protocol, and etiquettes. These behavioral elements comprise the company's unwritten code of conduct that will help you stay in the game.

## Endnotes

1. Janine Willis and Alexander Todorvo, "First Impressions, Making up Your Mind After a 100-Ms Exposure to a Face," *Psychological Science* 17, no. 7 (2006): 592–7.

2. http://lindatalleysblog.blogspot.com/2010_07_01_archive.html, accessed 5 July 2010.

# 3

# Giving Yourself Permission

La'Quisha did pretty well getting registered, putting on her name tag, and moving down the hallway to where she could look through the doorway and see people milling about, chatting, and visiting a long refreshment table along one wall. Then her feet turned into lead, and butterflies began to whirl around inside her—big sumo-wrestler-sized butterflies. This wasn't her thing at all.

A hostess just inside the door saw her pull up short, maybe saw her eyes widening. She smiled at La'Quisha and waved a hand to invite her inside.

La'Quisha took a few slow, leaden steps inside the doorway.

"There you go," the hostess said. "Now get out there and mingle—get to know some people better."

The crowd looked harmless enough—some people were even smiling. But for a second or two, La'Quisha thought of sharks swimming in a pool.

"You begin by beginning," La'Quisha thought. "Now, come on!" She took one step, then another. Before she knew it, she was talking to someone and trading business cards. Someone approached her, so she talked some more. This wasn't so bad. She moved through the crowd, joined a small group briefly, and then talked with three different people individually. Piece of cake. She even got into a conversation while moving along the refreshment table that introduced her to three more people and turned out to be one of the most productive moments of the evening.

Making that plunge had been the hardest part, but once La'Quisha got rolling, she was plowing through the milling throng, making new friends and contacts left and right. Being prepared made all the difference. She had to tip her hat to those Boy Scouts, whose motto is, "Be prepared!" There was a lot to be said for that.

Maybe you would feel the same at first, in a similar situation, and wonder, "How do I begin?" How would you have felt if you'd been in La'Quisha's place? For that matter, how do you feel in any similar situation, such as before class, before a school event or activity, or at any gathering when you have 15 minutes to "network" before things get started? What are you thinking when you attend a "networking" event at a school social function, convention, business meeting, class, or seminar? What is your attitude when you join a school club, voluntary membership organization, professional society, trade group, or other special interest group? Do any of the following thoughts run through your mind?

- How do I approach a classmate, peer, fellow delegate, or business associate and introduce myself?

- Is it up to me to keep the conversation going? If so, how do I do that?

- What if I'm the only new person and everyone else already knows each other? Will they think I'm pushy or intruding?

- How do I break the ice? What is the best or safest thing to say?

- How do I break away from someone so I can keep on mingling?

- How long should the first networking encounter last?

- What if someone asks me a question for which I don't know the answer?

Don't fret. You're not alone. Many people who attend events, social activities, seminars, and workshops express these same feelings about networking. Old habits die hard.

When you're not familiar with the simple techniques of effective networking, you naturally tend to stay within your comfort zone. Hanging out with friends or standing in the corner and waiting for the meal or event to begin is comfortable. Yes, even eating rubbery chicken seems better than talking to someone you don't know.

However, this isn't taking advantage of the opportunities at hand. Unless you're making new contacts all the time, your network isn't growing.

## Give Yourself Permission

You have to give yourself permission to network. Changing your attitude to a positive one is the first step to success. Just allowing yourself that "switch" in your mindset can make all the difference. Then you need some techniques you can immediately use when you walk into a room full of people or when someone announces, "It's time to network."

## Fourteen Easy Techniques for When "It's Time to Network"

Here are 14 easy-to-learn, easy-to-use techniques that you can immediately adopt to become an effective networker while you're a student.

1. Have a business card.

2. Have an "icebreaker" opening line.

3. Develop your "branding statement." Some people call this an "elevator statement" because you should be able to complete it on a short elevator ride. It's a 20- to 30-second infomercial about yourself that gives the listener a reason to pay attention to you.

4. Do your research and know something about your potential network associates.

5. Have a list of "get to know you" questions prepared and practiced so that you sound natural.

6. Develop a list of idea-generator topics (small talk).

7. Get in line.

8. Take a deep breath; visualize yourself engaged in a thoughtful, interesting, and memorable conversation; and dive into a group.

9. Look for a designated host or greeter, and start there.

10. If you and the contact have your hands free (no juggling of plates and glasses), extend your hand first and offer a firm (not bone-crushing or limp-wrist) handshake, and introduce yourself. Be sure to consciously talk slower than you normally would—your adrenalin is pumping, and you'll be talking faster than you think.

11. If you're seated at a table, start a conversation with the person to your right or left.

12. Have an exit strategy, a "break the contact" comment that allows you both to break off conversation gracefully.

13. Set a goal for every event or activity you attend to build your network by some number.

14. Follow up with a thank you.

## *Get and Use a Business Card*

Business cards might seem like an unnecessary expense that can wait. But that's just not true. Business cards are absolutely necessary for networking. If you want a person to remember you or ever contact you, a business card is a must. Online services such as Vista.com, overnightprints.com, 123print.com, and printcentric.com often offer a limited number of business cards for free or for a small fee. In addition, using Microsoft and other software programs, you can produce perfectly acceptable business cards on your own and print them on your own printer; your only expense is the card stock. Lastly, FedEx shipping stores, Office Depot, and Staples can print small quantities of cards (250 to 500) for less than $40.

If you're a college graduate and/or are not employed, you can design a European-style card, which displays your name, phone number, and perhaps email address centered on the card; you could add your mailing address if you want.

## *Have an Opening Line*

An opening line isn't a standard one-line-fits-all remark. For example, an opening line at a networking event isn't the same type of line you'd hear in a bar or at a party.

You can't use the same icebreaker in every situation, nor do you need a dozen different openings, like a set of different clubs for golf. Two or three variations should be sufficient to cover just about all the networking situations.

**Remember: Preparation and understanding the playing field are everything.**

The most important preparations you can make involve first thinking in advance about what you will say when you meet someone new. This means you need to prepare several different opening lines, or "icebreakers," and try them out on several people. Second, understand the psychology of human contact. By an overwhelming percentage (some experts say 90 percent or more), most human communications are nonverbal. So your initial contact and subsequent follow-up communications with another person will be predominately conducted through body language, tonality, and neurologic impressions.

Furthermore, we know from research (from a field called neuroplasticity) that people make microjudgments about other individuals they see and meet for the first time. These thin slices of rapid cognition constitute a major part of what we call intuition. Much of this takes place in our unconscious brains, but it's a powerful primer for whether you make a great or poor first impression on someone. The really good news is you have control over this primer. A natural, comfortable, and warm smile with a firm handshake is page one in this primer.

Remember that you not only have to develop these icebreakers, but you also have to practice, practice, practice. The idea is for your opening line to sound normal and conversational in the given situation, not awkwardly rehearsed or phony. For example, you should have one opening statement for a totally accidental and very brief meeting, such as in a hallway, in an elevator, or on an escalator. Have another opening statement ready for when you're seated next to a person, such as at a meal or in a meeting. A third opening statement to prepare is one you can use in a social gathering, such as a cocktail reception or trade show exhibit gathering.

An icebreaker is an *opening* and, as such, should focus on the other person, not you. You want to show empathetic skills right off the bat.

You're someone who cares about other people, their needs, their time, their problems, and their business. The more you use these opening lines, the easier they will flow and sound natural. As with any skill you practice, using these opening lines often will make them part of your conversation.

The following lines (preceded with a natural smile and, if appropriate, a handshake) are just some ideas for you to examine and customize for your own style.

- "Hello, my name is _____." You might consider adding "and I'm a junior analyst at _____" or "I'm a new employee at _____."

- "Are you a member? I'm thinking of joining this [group, organization, etc.]."

- "How have you found these [events, programs, activities, etc.]?"

- "What brought you out to this [event, meeting, activity, luncheon, etc.]?"

- "I'm new here. Can you tell me anything about this [group, organization, meeting, activity, etc.]?"

- "I'm interested in joining [or becoming a member of] this group, and this is my first [meeting, event, activity, etc.]. How does this compare to others you have attended?"

- "Have you attended this type of meeting before? What do you think about it?"

- "Have you heard the speaker before? What can you tell me about him or her?"

- "Could you tell me something about this [group, association, society, organization, firm, etc.]?"

- "You appear to know your way around this group. Could you please help me?"

- "I recognize you [or your company name]. Would you mind if I ask you a few questions about how you benefit from this [group, association, society, organization, firm, etc.]?"

Note that effective icebreakers are mostly open-ended questions. These are questions that require more than a specific one- or two-word answer. The opening line that can be answered with a "yes" or "no" response leaves you no closer to breaking the ice than before you spoke. The trick is to get the other person talking and to start a conversation. Then you will have broken the ice. Something else very important happens when you get the other person talking: Research has shown that people generally enjoy talking about themselves.

Furthermore, sociologists tell us that when two or more people are engaged in a conversation, the person who speaks least is thought of by the other participants as being more intelligent. In addition, listening empathetically helps you build rapport, which is commonly referred to as "chemistry" with the other person. Your new network contact will be much more responsive if he or she notices that you are actively acknowledging his or her comments.

Pay attention to the little things—they can make a major difference in how strongly you are able to connect with them. For example, most people love to hear their name repeated. You should repeat a person's name upon meeting or being introduced. This repetition of the name serves as a reminder both in your memory and as the positive first impression and helps you remember it. Mentioning the person's name subsequently in the conversation reinforces the prime and adds to the other person's positive feelings.

Notice what people say and what they're wearing. Look for clues about their interests and what things appeal to them so that these can become points of conversation later.

## Develop a Twenty- to Thirty-Second Branding Statement

Be prepared to introduce yourself and answer the question, "What do you bring to the conversation?" Of course, no one is going to say, "So _____, what do you bring to this conversation?" or "What can you do for me?" or "What can you do for my company?"

However, if you prepare as though that is what people really are thinking, you will be ready. Think of this as your 20- to 30-second infomercial. It should be clear, concise, enthusiastic (passionate is okay), and memorable. It should give the other person a benefit and encourage him or her to want to know more about you.

Most importantly, *your branding statement should demonstrate that you have the other person's interest, needs, or company in mind.* Remember, first impressions count, and you have a limited time (less than two seconds) to reinforce that first impression. Your branding statement is the key to opening the potential that can come from each contact. You have to build a branding statement just as you would create a mission statement, a goal, or an objective.

First, you have to develop a sound strategy. You need to take an introspective inventory of yourself, including a thorough review and analysis of your background, character, skill set, abilities, knowledge, intellect, interests, worldview, experiences—all the things that make you unique and differentiated.

Everyone on the planet is unique and differentiated, but we usually don't spend much time thinking about these differences. Many people were brought up to believe that they shouldn't talk about themselves. This kind of thinking is self-defeating; put it aside and spend enough time in self-evaluation to honestly and clearly articulate what makes you special.

You don't need to have a professional psychologist conduct a Myers-Briggs battery of tests to do a self-evaluation. After you've made a list of what makes you unique and special, you must create your branding statement around those traits.

## Develop a Sound S.T.R.A.T.E.G.Y. for Your Branding Statement

S    Make your infomercial **short** and **succinct**.

T    **Think** of it in advance.

R    **Remember** the **results** you want to achieve.

A    Be **articulate** in your message.

T    **Time** is of the essence—30 seconds is the maximum length.

E    Speak with **enthusiasm** and **energy**.

G    Set a **goal** to attain.

Y    Focus on **you** (the other person), not *me*.

## Do Your Research, and Know Something about Your Potential Network Associates

When you have a meeting or appointment scheduled with a networking associate, or if you have reason to believe that you will meet a key networking associate, research the person and his or her company or organization. Find out as much information as possible about the event you will be attending. The event, the company, and the individual will likely have press room pages, event home pages, news centers, or profiles on the Internet.

Also look through the history pages. Check hard-copy sources such as trade magazines, newspapers, and newsletters related to the individual and his or her industry. Search for any and all ways to differentiate yourself from every other contact your network associate meets. Any piece of information you have that shows your interest, knowledge, or initiative in this person's field begins to create rapport and could lead to the individual building interest in you.

## Have a List of "Get to Know You" Questions Prepared and Practiced So You Sound Natural

"Get to know you" questions are different from your opening statement or icebreakers, in that they focus on the person you're speaking to, not an event you're both attending or a situation you're both experiencing.

Here's a story about how a "get to know you" question works. Several years ago, Andrea was in London to give a workshop. When she entered the auditorium to set up, the room was full of people sitting quietly in their seats, staring straight ahead.

She asked them whether they were all waiting for her session to begin or whether they were still spellbound by the last session. She got a chuckle. As it turned out, they were waiting for her session, which wasn't scheduled to begin for another 20 minutes. Hearing this, Andrea responded, "Great, there's a chance to get to know your neighbors." It was as though they'd all been asked to make a presentation. No one moved. Finally, one man raised his hand and commented, "We don't do that over here." Andrea smiled and said that people don't do much of that in New York, either, yet it's a wonderful way to connect with someone, pass the time, and even learn something new about each other. Andrea knew that people love to follow instructions, so she asked each person to turn to a neighbor and ask the following questions:

- Why did you come to this conference?

- Where do you work, and what do you do?

- Where do you live?

- What other sessions have you attended?

- What do you do when you're not working?

- What do you love about your work?

- What type of projects do you get involved in, and what have you done recently?

At first, nothing happened. Then in about 30 seconds, they all started talking at once—and kept at it. Andrea said it was actually hard to get them to stop so she could start her session. When she asked, "Who just met someone interesting?" All hands went up. People wanted to share things they'd just learned, and they discovered that they had friends in common, interests in common, and even neighborhoods in common. More important to their business lives, they met colleagues who could help with their projects, they learned about parts of the company they'd never known about, and they learned how they could become a resource to others.

Develop your own set of personal and business-related "get to know you" questions. You can use the ones just mentioned as a guide. Add questions related to family, travel, hobbies, favorite books or movies, and other interests. Add business-related questions appropriate to the situation, and then try them out at the next gathering of business people you attend. We guarantee you'll meet someone interesting.

## *Develop a List of Idea-Generator Topics (Small Talk)*
Write down ideas as you think of them. Consider keeping a journal organized by topic. Become conversant about current affairs, best-selling books, top movies, business news, the stock market, global affairs, and certainly the latest news in certain key industries of interest to you.

Develop some opening lines around these topics:

- What did you think about the State of the Union speech?

- What business authors do you recommend?

- What business journals do you read?

- What kind of skills do you think hiring managers are looking for today versus ten years ago?

- How do you think the role of managers has changed as a result of the Internet?

- What has changed the most about the [industry or company] since you began?

- What do you think is different about the generation of workers today than the one before [or the one to come]?

## *Get in Line*

At any business or social event, there's usually a line at the bar, refreshment table, buffet table, registration desk, coat check—you name it. When you're standing in line, there's a natural opportunity to start a conversation with the person in front of or behind you. Here's an example of how networking while standing in line worked for Andrea. It was right before lunch, and there was a line in front of the ladies' room (where else?) at the hotel where Andrea was attending a meeting. Andrea noted the name tag of the woman in front of her and realized they would be in the same meeting.

Andrea opened the conversation with, "Have you been to these meetings before? And if so, what do you think of them?" As Andrea and the woman chatted, Andrea discovered that the woman was the vice president of a cable company. They exchanged business cards, and Andrea promised to send her information about her seminars. Within seven months, the woman had become a client—all because of a conversation begun while waiting for the restroom.

## Take a Deep Breath and Dive into a Group

At any gathering, groups form. Look for a group that looks friendly, wait for an opening, and say something like, "I don't mean to interrupt, but you seem like a friendly group. I'm new here. Would you mind if I joined you?" Who could say no to that? Often people will respond by saying something like, "That took courage—I admire that. It's nice to meet you."

Andrea, Michael, and Renee have been in situations, such as receptions or business affairs, when they were corralled by photographers to be part of a group photo for some magazine or newsletter. After smiling for the picture, you have a great opportunity to turn to the group and admit that you're new to the event, ask if they're members or have been before, and use your 30-second branding statement followed by a get-to-know-you question.

We know that approaching a group or an individual isn't easy the first few times. Even if you've done all the preparation we've suggested, it can still feel uncomfortable. So give yourself a pep talk! Write down a couple positive and interesting things about yourself, such as these:

- I am glad to be here.

- I am a great listener.

- I am friendly, and a great person, and eager to learn and meet new people.

- I am learning much about my field and already know a lot about _____.

Then in your mind's eye, visualize yourself successfully having the kind of networking conversation that will lead to a long-lasting favorable business relationship.

## Look for a Designated Host or Greeter and Introduce Yourself

At many functions, a host, greeter, or sponsor has the job of introducing you to others, especially if you're a new member or a guest visiting for the first time. Ask the host for help in meeting people.

## Introduce Yourself to the Speaker

If the event you're attending includes a speaker, take the opportunity to tell this individual how much you're looking forward to his or her talk. Mention something specific about the topic or the speaker (remember your research). After the presentation, follow up with a note saying how much you enjoyed the talk, and mention some helpful bit of information you took away.

## Start a Conversation with Your Meal Partner

At a seated meal, the person to your right or left is a logical person to engage. Use your icebreaker opening statements to start a conversation.

## Have an Exit Strategy

Even when you're engrossed in a great conversation with someone, it is perfectly polite to leave something for the next time and close your conversation with a follow-up plan so that you can move on and talk with someone else. The other scenario that calls for an exit strategy is when you're talking with someone and you find yourself mentally counting the minutes to get away. Here are some lines to practice:

- "It was great meeting you, and hopefully we can continue our conversation some other time."

- "Thanks for sharing the information about _____. It sounds exciting. Best of continued success."

- "Please excuse me—I see a friend I would like to go say hello to."

- "I've enjoyed hearing about _____. I'm sure we will speak again soon."

- "You've been very interesting to speak with. I'll let you have the opportunity to share your thoughts with some others."

## Set a Goal for Every Event or Activity You Attend

There's is an old saying in business: "To improve something, it first has to be counted and measured." If you want to get better at networking, you first have to set a goal for yourself. Then set a measurable standard that can be counted and measured toward that goal. We're not talking about a complicated evaluation process here—just something as easy as, "I want to improve my networking skills, and to do this, I will make four new contacts a week for the next three months." Just to give you an idea of how powerful this simple goal and standard is, if you were to achieve just 50 percent of this, you would make 25 new networking affiliations.

### *Follow Up with a Note or a Thank You Note, If Appropriate*

You can never go wrong by sending a handwritten note to a new networking contact—especially a thank you note, when appropriate. This one act will differentiate you more than almost anything you can do.

## Summary

These 14 techniques will help you get through any networking event with confidence. When you start practicing and applying them, you will find yourself actually looking forward to networking events as you continue to expand your network and enrich your life.

# 4

# Creating Connections: The People You Will Need in Your Network

The recurring theme we hear is, "African Americans don't help each other and we don't know that many people who can help us." When we hear this, we are reminded of these words of Henry Ford: "You can believe that you can succeed or you can believe you can fail. Either way, you'll be right." This is looking at the glass as being half full. Unless you have been living on an uninhabited desert island for your entire life up to this moment, you know a lot more people than you think you do. These people, some of whose names you may have to think a little to remember, will become the core of your created network.

Your coworkers, colleagues, and organization affiliates (such as church or club members) should supply a rich source of networking contacts for you. Many black people aren't comfortable seeking network contacts, but their workplace and churches are good places to start and succeed because of the small world theory. You might have heard the theory stated in terms of "six degrees of separation," meaning that just about everyone you meet is within six contacts of knowing everyone else. The key here is that people have more contacts than they are aware of, and if they take the time to make these contacts effective assets, the effort will pay off for them and their contacts.

Networking is not just for networking events or for when we're told, "It's time to network." *Networking is a way of life, a state of mind.* We do it all the time without even realizing it.

In this chapter, you explore how to identify the types of people you want to include in your network. You will discover that many of them are already in your life. But you might be saying, "I don't have time to network. I'm already too busy to be with my friends and do the things I want to do!" Sound familiar? Read on to learn how these people and activities fit right into your busy life and can be part of your networking success story.

## Types of People for Your Network

An important first step for you is to identify the people with whom you want to build a relationship. You need these types of people in your network:

- Fellow coworkers and colleagues
- Individuals you've met at seminars, workshops, and conferences
- Coworkers at your last job(s)
- Relatives
- Friends
- Neighbors
- People you meet by chance, such as while standing in lines or waiting for buses or trains
- Like-minded people
- Medical practitioner(s)
- Retail sales clerks and the merchants you buy from
- Ministers
- People in your address books (instant message, BlackBerry, and cellphone contacts, as well as contacts from Facebook and other social networking sites)
- People on your Christmas card list
- People you met at the last five parties you attended
- People at your gym or spa
- Sports teammates
- The service, repair, and maintenance people who come to your home
- Your barber or hairdresser

- Every professional with whom you come into contact

- Waitresses and waiters

- Members of your church or membership clubs

- Fellow pet owners

- Fellow gamers

# It's a Small World

The truth is, almost everyone with whom you come into contact—friends, graduates, family members, coworkers—knows someone you can learn something from to potentially benefit your job search, your personal life, or even your hobbies and interests.

# Weak Tie Theory

We've all heard the phrase, "It's not what you know, but who you know." In 1974, Mark Granovetter developed a theory that he called the Weak Tie Theory (WTT). Many researchers reviewed, studied, and reexamined the WTT during the past 25 years. Most have confirmed Granovetter's original results that job seekers have two groups in which to network. Granovetter refers to the first group as "strong ties," consisting of family members, friends, peers, and fellow members of churches, clubs, and other groups. These individuals in the strong network are people the job seeker sees and speaks with on a fairly regular basis. Granovetter claims that the strong network can be helpful and supportive, but the job seeker receives too much repetitive information from this group. The strong network knows the same people, so this group has very little unique information about new job opportunities.

The second group, which Granovetter refers to as "weak ties," consists of individuals the job seeker does not know and probably has never met. The weak network provides the job seeker with nonrepetitive information and frequently has new information about jobs that the original job seeker doesn't know. The actual hiring manager is part of the weak network. *Getting into the weak network becomes the key to taking advantage of its great strength.*

---

The weak network is simply people you do not have regular contact with—friends of friends and their friends, people who have nonrepetitive industry and job information and who are likely to be outside your industry, and people you don't normally associate with frequently. These are people you wouldn't normally know; others closer to you would have to make the introduction. Likewise, weak ties are often people other networkers (in your strong tie network) would not know or ordinarily network with—hence, *weak* network.

The weak network is critical because your greatest job opportunities lie here. Make no mistake, people do get job opportunities using only their strong networks. However, the opportunities for the jobs with the greatest prestige, status, compensation potential, and career growth are likely to be found within your weak ties.

Networking within weak tie networks is done exactly the same way it is done in strong networks. To effectively network, you must stay connected and build upon both your strong and *weak* ties. It is imperative to nurture both relationships, to maintain social connectivity. Often people stay connected with others in their immediate circle or those of the same race, but the people we are weakly tied to and who move in different circles from our own are the ones who have different information that could be valuable to us when job searching. We typically get crucial information from people whose existence we have forgotten until a happenstance meeting occurs.[1]

According to Gregory and Jeffrey[2], often African Americans are disconnected from the web of social relationships that might connect them with those who are in hiring positions, especially in smaller firms. One reason for the disconnection is that African Americans are underrepresented among firm owners and hiring managers. Blacks make up approximately 13 percent of the U.S. population, but only 4 percent of firm owners are black.[3] Although being connected to a web of social relationships is helpful, it's not absolutely necessary to have a personal connection to conduct a successful job search—still, it might be useful to "know someone" or "know someone who knows someone." Having an acquaintance or personal referral is an advantage in the job seeker's social network.[4]

Troy Tassier confirms that acquaintances can be valuable job contacts. He agreed with Granovetter that acquaintances are weak ties (compared to close friends, who are considered strong ties). Tassier reported that studies have successfully shown weak ties are a common and important source of finding employment.[5]

How do you strengthen your weak ties to the web of social networking? You'll find many tips throughout this book, including Fairchild and Robinson's[6] recommendation of participating in organizations and institutions that give you access to higher-status individuals.

## Summary

Most African-American professionals have more contacts than they think they have. If they cultivate these contacts with their social networking skills, they will gain a head start in networking.

## Endnotes

1. Mark Granovetter, *Getting a Job, a Study of Contact and Careers,* 2d ed. (Chicago: University of Chicago Press, 1974).

2. Gregory B. Fairchild and Jeffrey Robinson, *It's What You Know and Who They Know: Weak Ties and Strong Ties in Urban Labor Markets*, Academy of Management Conference Paper, 2004.

3. Small Business Administration, 2001.

4. Fairchild and Robinson, 2004.

5. Troy Tassier, "Labor Market Implications," *Southern Economic Journal 72*, no. 3 (2006): 704–19.

6. Fairchild and Robinson, 2004.

# 5

# Characteristics of Great Networkers

**D**o you know someone who can walk into a room full of strangers and immediately make friends? Can you recall someone who instantly made you feel at ease when you first met him or her? How about a person who makes you feel as though you are the only person in the world when he or she is speaking to you?

If you know such a person, or multiple people, take a moment to think about what personality traits they possess. Are they confident? Empathetic? Enthusiastic? Energetic? Tenacious? Caring? Appreciative? As you have already noted, they're good listeners. Chances are, they possess all these qualities—and more. You can possess these characteristics as well, and this chapter focuses on how.

Here you look at each characteristic and discuss how it works in effective networking. You should adapt these skills to your own personality, lifestyle, worldview, abilities, and goals as you develop your own networking skills.

Effective networkers are people who connect because they are:

1. Confident

2. Empathetic

3. Appreciative

4. Tenacious

5. Enthusiastic and energetic

6. Caring

7. Rapport builders

Networking and success are not disconnected, and it's no quirk or coincidence that so many successful people have large, diverse networks. Evidence suggests that the one common characteristic of successful people in many different fields, professions, and walks of life is that they've all built large personal networks. Networking alone won't make someone successful. However, without a network, a person isn't likely to achieve a high level of success.

Consider the seven characteristics of successful people detailed in the next sections.

## Confidence

Justin is the president of a runner's club that meets for runs on Saturday mornings. He exudes confidence. It shows in the simplest of matters, such as how he can silence 50 eager runners to make announcements or muster an army of volunteers to raise thousands of dollars for a run to benefit cancer research. His confidence is magnetic. People gravitate to him and eagerly offer their time and expertise.

Where did Justin's confidence come from? You can't buy it. If a store did sell it, we'd all be in line to buy. *Confidence comes with experience and grows over time.* What kind of experience helps us develop it? Not sitting still. Not doing the same thing repeatedly and expecting different results. To build confidence, you have to step out of your comfort zone and take some risks. It helps to start with small steps and then keep going as your confidence grows.

You can join organizations, go to meetings, take part in committees, do planning work, join boards, and volunteer to speak, particularly in clubs such as Toastmasters and American Marketing Association chapters.

The more active you become, the more confidence you develop in your ability to meet others and speak up.

In Chapter 11, "Tying It All Together," you meet Darius, one of Michael's students. He had to step out from his comfort zone to meet and follow up with the people with whom he wanted to connect. He took small steps, made a plan, and before long was choosing between two excellent job offers. Darius would be the first to tell you he was less than comfortable at first, even reluctant, but he persisted; the more he tried networking, the better he got. Soon he was confident in his ability to meet and talk with people, and people were eager to meet him. His confidence made him more relaxed and approachable.

Compare this process to any new skill you have mastered, such as learning to play tennis or video games or speaking in front of a group. You started with small steps and progressed as your competence and confidence grew. Most important, you had to step outside your comfort zone, take a risk, and do something different. As you continued to practice and got better at the skill, you gained confidence. Did you also notice that people were more interested in what you had to say than before? Expanding your contacts in your field of expertise was suddenly easier.

To develop confidence, practice the skills you want to attain. Over time, the confidence you have developed in your abilities will show. As with Darius, people will be drawn to you because you've become a more confident person.

## Empathy

An empathetic person puts him- or herself in another person's shoes. Being empathetic doesn't necessarily mean you share another's point of view; it does, however, mean you are concerned about others and interested in hearing their point of view. Some people confuse empathy with sympathy, but they are not the same. Consider the difference: When you listen to someone with a sympathetic view, you feel a *temporary* uneasiness for the individual, but it doesn't reach the level of impacting you personally. In contrast, listening to someone with an empathetic view leaves you with the exact same feeling—good or bad—as the speaker, and you can easily see yourself in the exact same position.

Empathetic people pay attention to the details. They take the time to look and listen to others. They observe and interpret body language. They listen as carefully to what people leave unsaid as to what they say. They have the ability to read between the lines. They can tell when a friend is preoccupied and respect these boundaries. They have the ability to make other people truly feel that they are heard and valued.

For an example, consider a situation Andrea experienced. She was working at home when she received a call from a business colleague, Susan.

Although Susan tried to sound upbeat, Andrea could tell something wasn't quite right. Susan's voice and speech pattern didn't seem normal. Susan didn't want to discuss anything over the phone, which Andrea respected. However, Andrea suggested coffee the next morning. Susan then confided she'd lost her job in a sudden dismissal and was in a state of shock and depression.

Andrea listened, observed, and encouraged Susan to begin working on a career plan. Within a week, Andrea received a call from another contact who was looking for a person with skills similar to those of Susan. A few calls and a meeting or two later, and Susan had a new job and career. Andrea's empathetic skills set the ball in motion to make other things happen.

How different people communicate—how they give and receive information—is an important part of how they view themselves. Empathetic people are aware of communication styles and adapt their style to others when appropriate. Part of adapting a style involves understanding that we all use different styles of communication when giving and receiving information.

Some people are auditory. They learn and communicate best through listening and case discussion. They learn best by hearing information. They prefer a verbal report over a written report. They like to listen to the news rather than read a newspaper. When speaking with an auditory-type person, it makes sense to check in with the person using phrases such as, "Are we in harmony?," "Are we connecting?," "Are we in sync?," or "How does this sound to you?"

Some people are visual. They learn through watching, observing, and reading. They need to see images, or "see it in writing." These are the folks who take lots of notes in lectures and treasure the handouts. These people love visuals, PowerPoints and other types of presentations, and flipcharts. When visual-type individuals communicate, they often draw what they're talking about on a pad or whiteboard. To connect with them, you might use phrases such as, "How does this look to you?" or "Picture this...."

The third major learning approach is kinesthetic—learning through doing, practicing, or touching. These people need to act things out or have things demonstrated to them. They're likely to talk with a lot of hand and arm motion, gestures, and animation. They learn best by actually doing or taking part. Check phrases for these people might include, "Are you comfortable with this?" or "How does this feel to you?"

In addition to being aware of communication styles, empathetic people adjust themselves to other people's orientation. Some people are more oriented or sensitive to the concerns and feelings of others; other people are more "bottom line," or results oriented; and still others are interested and concerned with details and the way things work.

Obviously, this is a simplification of the complex concept of personality styles and behavior types. Study this concept if you're interested; however, to be empathetic, all you really need to do is listen carefully and respect the other person's orientation. While listening, pay attention to what people are saying—and not saying. Look at their facial impressions and determine whether their verbiage is congruent. For example, if someone indicates that it's a pleasure to meet you but has a frown on her face, clearly the message is confusing. Be careful about the message you send. Smiling is a universal sign; the more you smile, the more approachable you are.

Andrea once presented a business proposal to three different decision makers within a single organization. She knew from previous conversations that she was dealing with three different personality styles.

The human resources director was harmonious and amiable in her approach. She had mentioned to Andrea that she wanted to "make sure to get everyone involved." Caring and concern were important, as was emphasizing the human element. In this case, Andrea had to focus her presentation on the personal benefits for the employees. The chief financial officer, on the other hand, was primarily interested in the return on investment he would get from Andrea's program. He also wanted a lot of details. In this presentation, the more detailed the data, the better the client liked it. The chief executive officer, the third individual, only had five minutes to give Andrea. All he wanted to know was, "What are my people going to learn?" and "How much is it going to cost?" In this presentation, Andrea just answered those two questions, for a short succinct "bottom line" summary. In this case, three very different people all wanted basically the same information, but in vastly different ways.

For Andrea to succeed, she had to deliver the information in the way each person needed it. An empathetic person is an excellent listener who understands and adapts to the needs of others.

Being empathetic doesn't mean you have to change your personality, of course, nor does it necessitate being solicitous, weak, or manipulative. It's a positive, sincere, and proactive approach to understanding someone else's feelings, interests, and needs. The dictionary definition of *empathy* is "the action of understanding [and] being aware of...the feelings, thoughts, and experience of another...without having the feelings, thoughts, and experience fully communicated in an objectively explicit manner." Therefore, to become empathetic, you need to be aware of communication styles and personality types.

# Appreciation

The quality that makes people more charismatic networkers is their natural instinct to give sincere appreciation. You can never tell someone "thank you" too many times when you do so sincerely. You can say thank you in many ways, but the most effective way, according to most surveys on the topic, is the handwritten note sent via the U.S. Postal Service.

These days, digital technology enables you to use a font that appears handwritten even though the note is typed; thus, you gain the efficiency of digital communications and the personalization of the U.S. Postal Service. You can send thank you notes by email, which is quick, easy, and immediate. However, the recipient can delete messages even before they're opened, so there is a chance that your note might not even be seen. A handwritten note, on the other hand, is unlikely to be discarded before it is read. There's also the face-to-face thank you, delivered sincerely and with special emphasis on the communication style of the person you are appreciating. You can also show your appreciation by sending a small gift.

Saying thank you might seem like rather simple etiquette—a no-brainer—yet it's amazing how few people remember to take the action and how positive an impact the action has when taken. It can do wonders for your professional and personal growth as a networker.

# Tenacity

At least 20 percent of Andrea's business has come from people who turned her down the first time. When Andrea realized this, she saw it as a lesson that being tenacious can pay off for networking and for business.

Andrea recalls how tough one current customer was to win over. She called on this client for three years and went nowhere. No one even returned her calls. The direct approach clearly was not working, so she decided to network her way to the client. Andrea thought about the client and what organizations, events, activities, and clubs this client might belong to or attend. An old saying applies to this strategy: "If you want blueberries, go to where the blueberries grow." So Andrea went to where the blueberries grew. She belonged to several business networking groups and thought it might be possible the client would attend one of these groups.

At least, Andrea reasoned, if the client didn't attend, someone from her firm might attend. The break came when Andrea was giving a presentation at a meeting of one of the groups. After the presentation, a woman from the target client's firm approached and suggested Andrea meet with someone in her firm who could use Andrea's services. The woman offered to set up the meeting. Guess who that someone turned out to be? None other than Mrs. Never Returns My Calls. The story does not have a happy ending yet, though.

Andrea and the prospective client did meet, but Andrea could tell the woman was doing it out of courtesy for her coworker and really didn't want to meet with her. However, things got better as the meeting progressed; it ultimately went past the original 20 minutes the woman had allotted and lasted an hour and a half. At the end of the meeting, the woman told Andrea that she liked the proposal but, frankly, it took five years for outside consultants to land work in the firm. She did tell Andrea to call quarterly, just to stay in touch. At first Andrea was discouraged—but at least she'd gotten in the door. Now she had five years to go, so she'd better hang in there.

Andrea sent a handwritten thank you note, and a month later, when the woman was promoted, Andrea sent a note of congratulations.

When the first quarter was up, Andrea called and left this message: "I know I still have four and three-quarters years left. I am just touching base." Andrea continued to keep in touch for two quarters—and then, to her surprise, the woman called. Andrea was awarded not one, but two projects with the firm. In the time since, Andrea has done more than 30 projects for this firm, and it's one of her largest clients. Tenacity paid off. Instead of getting discouraged about the five-year timetable, Andrea just put it on her schedule to call every quarter and stayed in touch. Tenacity and patience sometimes make good partners.

When Michael was nearing the end of his active duty in the U.S. Marine Corps, he took advantage of a training program and became a licensed 35-mm motion picture projector operator. He worked his last few months in the Marines running a base movie theater projector operation in the evenings. He knew he was going to college upon his discharge, and the new skill offered a possible job while going to school.

According to union scale, motion picture projector operators were very well paid. Michael was discharged from the Marines and returned to St. Louis to begin community college. As it turned out, the union opportunities in the movie theaters were very lucrative, but only if your family was in the business already. Michael took his skill to a private professional audiovisual firm and worked for that firm while attending community college. Michael kept in contact with the president of that firm even when he moved to New Jersey to continue work on his bachelor's degree. Upon graduating from college, Michael returned to St. Louis. He contacted the president of the audiovisual firm, who said he was happy to give Michael whatever temp work he could. It was clear, though, that Michael was way overqualified for anything full time.

A week after returning, Michael got a call from the regional sales manager of the Dun & Bradstreet (D&B) office, who told him he was the next-door neighbor of the president of the audiovisual firm. The two men had been talking over their backyard fence the night before, and the D&B manager had mentioned how much he needed someone but didn't want to put out a "general casting call." The president of the audiovisual firm had given him Michael's resume, and the manager had made the call. Michael went in for the interview and was hired that day. He then spent 20 years with D&B. Tenacity and patience were partners once again.

One additional story strengthens the point about keeping up your networking even within your organization. Michael was very disciplined about extending his networking inside D&B because the same rules and opportunities apply inside a firm as they do to your general network. After ten years, Michael left D&B for another career opportunity with the Direct Marketing Association (DMA). Several years later, he returned to D&B through a contact with an individual he had kept in his network.

After five years, he took a buyout with several thousand other employees but returned a month later to a different D&B division, again as a result of a networking contact. All in all, he spent 20 years with D&B. When he left D&B for the last time, he moved to a senior position, by way of a networking contact, back to DMA.

So team up tenacity with patience, and keep your options open. Each move to each organization resulted in a promotion, more compensation, and a wider, more fulfilling network. There's a fine line between being tenacious and being a pest, though—be careful not to cross the line. Much of it has to do with getting permission to keep in touch. In the "five-year case," Andrea knew her initial meeting had gone well, and because the woman had invited her to keep in touch, it was appropriate to follow up with the phone calls and notes. Being tenacious is a positive way of taking advantage of opportunities, as well as looking at the setbacks that come along as opportunities in disguise and yet keeping at it.

It might seem counterintuitive, but we know from research and experience that people who are asked for help, if they do decide to help, will take a deep personal interest in the person who asked. It is as though they have an emotional and psychological investment in the person and want to protect their investment and ensure that it pays off. Being tenacious (and not pushy) is giving people something in which they can invest and engage.

# Enthusiasm and Energy

Enthusiasm and energy are contagious. When you're enthusiastic, you bring out the enthusiasm in others. If you're full of energy, the energy in the space around you rises. If you need proof, watch what happens at a gathering when folks are waiting for a speaker to take the floor. If the speaker arrives with energy, watch how the expressions on the audience's faces change and the room becomes "charged."

The experiment with one person controlling the mood of a group has been conducted so often that the results have become rather predictable. In control groups, one person is preselected to be either a mood depressor or a mood elevator. All it takes is one person with the right dynamics, and that one person can change the mood of an entire group in either a positive or negative direction. Jury selection experts have known about this dynamic for years and know that one person can project a certain mood or feeling, and the first "straw" vote is an excellent indicator of the final jury vote.

Viewed in a positive way, you can alter the impression people have of your intelligence just by your level of enthusiasm. High levels of enthusiasm are often mistaken for high levels of intelligence. By being highly enthusiastic, you not only raise the level of enthusiasm of others around you, but you also increase the possibility that others believe you are more intelligent than you are. There's nothing wrong with that! Enthusiasm also makes people more receptive to your message. Realize, though, that enthusiasm and energy come in many forms.

You don't have to be loud and excited to be energetic or enthusiastic. Enthusiasm can be a quiet passion that shines and makes people want to be a part of it.

# Caring

When you truly care about others and you don't expect a payback for your efforts, you will indeed get the ultimate reward. You will make others feel good about themselves and about you. Often the very act of caring will produce unexpected, positive networking results.

Recently, Andrea received one of those "voices from your past" phone calls. It was from Gloria, who had been the receptionist at a company

Andrea had called on years ago to sell advertising space. It had been 14 years since Andrea had last seen her. Gloria was now the vice president of marketing for another company. She had recently read an article Andrea had written and decided to call about doing a project for her new company. Andrea was flattered by the call and her invitation to do the project. When Andrea asked what had made her call, Gloria said that Andrea had always made her feel important when visiting the firm; Andrea had even told the then-president of the firm that Gloria had a great voice and a smile that truly came across on the phone.

Gloria told Andrea she'd always wanted to return the kindness, but as far as Andrea was concerned, there was no favor to be returned. Effective networkers are always networking not because they *need* to; rather, they network to create lifelong connections with people. They embrace networking as a way of life. They network without the thought of getting an immediate or specific payback.

Effective networkers know they're making positive connections in which all parties ultimately benefit. How very different this is from the image many people hold of "pathological networkers" who engage in "negative networking." These individuals never think of picking up the telephone, writing a personal note, sending an email, or extending a helping hand until they need something. They're not really networking.

## Rapport Building

Have you ever just met someone face-to-face and felt an instant bond, or been introduced to someone in a group and felt somehow "connected" with that person more than others in the group? That spontaneous or instant appeal is called rapport. It's identified by both verbal and non-verbal body language. The verbal communications include forms of agreements and elaborations and requests for more information. Showing rapport with language includes such phrases as these:

- "I see what you mean."
- "I understand."
- "I get the picture."
- "I hear what you're saying."

- "That sounds right to me."

- "That rings true to me."

- "That clicks with me."

- "That resonates with me."

- "I like your idea."

- "It makes sense to me."

The person wanting to show rapport may also probe with questions such as these:

- "Could you elaborate on that point?"

- "Can you clarify that?"

- "I would like to know more about that. Could you be more specific?"

- "Could you break that down into smaller pieces for me?"

- "Could you walk me through that again?"

Nonverbal body language includes more intense eye contact, head and upper-body movement toward you, open hand gestures, smiles, and light hand touching of the arm or shoulders.

Rapport is critical because it leads to influence and is a natural bridge to networking and the other six behavior patterns of people who are effective networkers.

## Selecting and Working with Mentors

One of the most valuable experiences you can receive is a mutually beneficial affiliation with an experienced network of qualified, professional, motivated mentors. The classic old-school model of the mentor–protégé relationship was based upon a senior executive selecting a junior colleague to take under his or her wing. Under this networking model, the protégé was guided in job choices, career direction, promotion options, business etiquette and culture, and even social and lifestyle issues.

The traditional mentor remained close to the protégé throughout the younger person's career. Often the two careers were linked.

Today the model has changed dramatically. Mentors and protégés still exist, but the environment of the classic model has all but disappeared. The executives of today's flatter, faster-paced organizations don't have the time or resources to support protégés. In addition to living a more hurried business life, many business executives have to pay renewed attention to their own careers.

Furthermore, today's African-American professionals don't need advice on achieving long-term success within specific organizations or industries. The focus is on their personal development in a changing working environment and an evolving economic climate. African-American professionals know that one person cannot help with all the issues, questions, and networking needed today. Therefore, the more practical approach for the contemporary protégé is a stable of mentors. Instead of being selected by a senior executive, today's protégé needs to take control of the process and seek out a team of mentors in different fields, specialties, knowledge areas, disciplines, professions, and industries.

With this approach, the black professional gains a heterogeneous and diverse set of opinions, views, and recommendations that meet the situational circumstances of today's young workers—which can and do change rapidly.

To begin building a stable of mentors, recognize that they do not have to be a separate group from your regular network—just individuals you've identified and targeted for extra-special attention. Certain special skills will be called on to develop this mentor group, such as being tenacious, enthusiastic, and effective at building rapport. The key in adapting to the current model is the emphasis on the protégé being proactive. All the rules and techniques we mention apply to mentor selection, but we want to emphasize how important it is to be proactive.

You are in a competitive environment. No one is going to "discover" you. No one will suddenly become aware of your great potential, approach you, and volunteer to mentor you. You must initiate the contact and reach out to those whose help you want. You are competing not only with your peers, but also for the time and resources of the targeted mentor. You cannot be coy or shy about identifying and approaching someone who will be willing to support your career development and give you advice, feedback, information, insight, and other forms of help. Pay close attention to how a contact relates and builds rapport with you.

If you pick up on signs that the person is willing to be helpful, test the waters with requests for information and advice to see how he or she responds. Without being overbearing, you need to be tenacious about starting and building a protégé–mentor relationship. You might need to take a more assertive lead in setting up planned meetings, such as coordinating specific days, times, and places for coffee or meals.

Don't be afraid to take a leadership position and offer to make arrangements for the meeting from which you will be gaining great benefit. Of course, in a mentor–protégé relationship, the frequency of contact is greater than in the normal networking relationship.

However, don't confuse simple instant messages (IM) or text messages to be mentor–protégé contacts. Messages sent frequently but with no real purpose other than real-time communications for the sake of real-time communications aren't the same thing.

When you do meet your mentor in person or online, make sure you've researched and responded to his or her previous requests. Always follow up and remind your mentor that you've found what he or she requested. Of course, it's better to have found *more* and to have exceeded your mentor's expectations.

Whenever possible, try to share personal information with your mentor. The one thing that hasn't changed in the mentor–protégé relationship is that once a person accepts the mentor's role, he or she feels personally responsible for the protégé's success. The mentor appreciates information and details that provide a connection to his or her role. You don't have to share intimate personal details or secrets, but do share information that opens a bridge and helps create a stronger bond.

Finally always be personable and enthusiastic. Mentors, like almost everyone else, prefer to work with people who exude a positive attitude.

# Summary

When you have developed and practiced the traits of an effective networker and you suddenly find yourself in a job hunt situation or needing a business contact, business leads, or other business assistance, you will have no problem contacting people who will be glad to lend you a helping hand. They will listen and offer sound advice, opportunities, and real referrals. Nonstop networking does work. Make nonstop networking your way of life.

# 6

# When Networking Doesn't Come Easy: Networking for Introverts

The more you network, the more you come into contact with different types of personalities and their varying styles of networking. Two very different types of personalities can approach a room full of people from completely different perspectives and achieve the same results.

One can work the room in a gregarious manner, meeting many different people and engaging in multiple conversations. Another can be quieter, engaging in fewer, more engrossed conversations. However, when they walk out of the meeting, they both have found new contacts, made new friends, made contacts, and secured referrals and leads.

The differences in their approach to networking are a result of their personality traits. The first person, the gregarious one, is more of an extrovert; extroverts get their energy from being around and interacting with people. The second person is more of an introvert; introverts gather their energy internally.

## The Introvert's Networking Advantage

Many introverts are good networkers. They know how to use their introverted nature to their advantage. They are often good listeners. They notice details and remember important facts, and because introverts often let others do more talking, the other person walks away thinking the introvert was a brilliant conversationalist.

Research and experience confirm that when one person has done the majority of the listening, both the speaker and people who have observed the conversation believe that the listener is the more intelligent of the two.

Introverts are also more thoughtful and frequently the first to give compliments, to remember special events, and, of course, to remember to say thank you. Think back to the last chapter and the critical importance of the six characteristics of great networkers. Three of the characteristics are common in introverts: empathy, appreciation, and caring. So if you are, or you suspect you are, an introvert, the first step is to understand and appreciate your best qualities—and then learn how to use them to your advantage in networking.

## Thoughtful Listening

Listening carefully to others is a skill most extroverts need to work on. It comes easier to introverts, who naturally absorb and use what they hear. Introverts generally spend more time listening and less time talking. Andrea knows a really great communicator named Alice. Every time they meet, Alice mentions something she remembers about Andrea from a prior conversation. Not long ago, Andrea and Alice were meeting about a project when Alice began a conversation by asking about Andrea's sister, Meredith, and her horse, Noddy.

Not only did Alice remember Andrea's sister's name, but she also remembered that she had a horse and knew the horse's name. Alice is an example of an excellent listener. She remembers details and puts the skill to work effectively. She is someone who epitomizes what we call a good networker. She listens, takes in all sorts of information, and when the time is right, puts together different people and projects where she thinks there's a good fit. If she were asked, Alice would say she is a total introvert and not a good networker. But she's wrong. Andrea thinks differently. Introverts can take advantage of their listening skills to build sound relationships, which is at the heart of being a good networker.

Some listening behaviors are important to be aware of so you can avoid them in your practice to become a good listener.

Most people are in one of two stages during a conversation: speaking or waiting to speak. Waiting to speak is a bad listening habit. If you're waiting to speak, then you're thinking about what you want to say, which means you're not listening. Here are some other common bad listening habits to avoid:

- Focusing on the other speaker instead of what he or she is actually saying

- Ignoring or shutting out what you don't understand or don't like

- Letting your emotions bias or filter what the other person is saying

- Daydreaming or letting external environmental factors distract you

- Interrupting before the speaker is finished

Good listeners engage in active emphatic listening. Normal American conversational speech is about 25 words per minute. Normal comprehension, on the other hand, can occur at 400 to 500 words per minute. In other words, you are capable of listening at a rate three to four times faster than the other person is capable of speaking.

This is nothing to celebrate. It's the reason for the most common bad listening habit: daydreaming. When you listen to someone speaking at a speed that's only about a third of your listening capability, your mind tends to fill its leftover capacity with other things.

These other things can then crowd out the conversation, and you lose some of what's being said. The cure for this inevitable tendency of the mind to wander during conversation is a discipline called active listening. Active listening is a way of giving your mind jobs to do that are concerned with the conversation. These jobs keep it focused. The following are three techniques you might want to consider as skill builders for better listening.

## First Listening Technique: Playing Back

One of the most powerful listening strategies is the technique of playing back. Listen to what the other person says, and play it back. It is particularly useful in a networking situation for introverts because it helps you check your interpretation of what the other person has said, and it makes that other person feel good. Beyond that, however, playing back is powerful because it forces you to process what the other person says. You can't simply repeat the other person's own words, although you sometimes may want to do that. To keep the conversation moving, you need to deal with *the meaning of what the other person says*. Playing back has the additional benefit of opening up the other person. Everyone has a desire to be understood, and playing back what the other person has said almost invariably encourages the person to provide additional information.

## Second Listening Technique: Summarizing

Summarizing is like playing back, except that it happens less frequently and involves more than one thought. As you process what the other person is saying, fit it together so you can summarize a list of points the person has made. As with playing back, this technique has benefits at two different levels:

1. It lets you check your understanding.

2. It forces you to attend to what the other person is saying so you can create the summary later.

At various points in the conversation, use a lead-in phrase and then list the points the other person has made: "If I have heard you correctly, you believe...."

Summarizing shows the other person that you're listening, and that's an important part of building the relationship.

## Third Listening Technique: Reflecting Emotion

Reflecting is a form of playing back, but *it applies to emotions rather than facts*. Whenever you hear a sign of emotion in the other person's conversation, you might want to acknowledge it. This shows the other person that you are attending to him or her as a person, and it builds your relationship.

One of the best lead-in phrases for reflecting emotion is "It sounds like...." For example, you might say, "It sounds like you're angry about the way that turned out." But you can use other phrases for variety, too, such as these:

- "I get the sense you're...."
- "I hear _____ in your voice."

## Passion

Many introverts don't relish the idea of walking up to a stranger and starting a conversation, but when they reach a topic they're passionate about, their shyness magically disappears. When you can focus on an aspect of business or a product or service you are especially passionate about, you will naturally speak with enthusiasm and conviction. Andrea recalls a conversation with an account executive who told her he became so nervous before meeting with a prospective client that he felt nauseous. Yet as soon as he started talking about his product, whose benefits he truly believed in, he felt comfortable and at ease. Introverts need a focus and a genuine reason to make a contact.

# Eleven Networking Techniques for the Quiet Networker

Under certain circumstances, most of us do feel shy, reticent, or introverted, regardless of what label you put on it. Half of us feel shy all the time—and the other half feel shy part of the time.

We've all felt stuck in the doorway thinking, "Should I walk into that crowded room at a meeting, seminar, workshop, or conference, or go back to my hotel room [or home]?" Yet we know that one key component of successful networking is visibility. You can't get visibility in a hotel room at a conference or at home unless you're networking over the Internet (more on that later in this chapter).

*Networking is all about making connections, building relationships, and developing advocates*, people who know us and know both what we do and what we are capable of doing so that they can become our marketers. Here are 11 tips on how to successfully network even when you're feeling introverted.

# 1. Have an Objective

Be truthful with yourself. Too much self-improvement advice begins with "goal setting" only. No progress is ever achieved because goals are long term, are ethereal in nature, and have no quantitative measurements.

Instead, set *objectives*, which are short term, goal oriented, measurable, and meaningful. Set goals for opportunities you have to expand or to nurture your network, and then set achievable measurable objectives.

- When attending a networking event, set an objective to meet and follow up with at least two people. By "follow up," we mean that you send a follow-up email or make a follow-up telephone call within a week.

- At school or university, set an objective to sit next to someone new. Think of three questions you can ask to learn about each person and his or her background and interests.

- Once a week, go through your contact list or social networking resource, and set an objective to select four to six individuals to email or call. The contacts should be individuals you haven't heard from recently. Use the opportunity to "check in" to say hello and ask both how they're doing and what they're doing.

- Set an objective to once a month have breakfast or lunch with a friend, colleague, or associate, particularly someone you haven't seen for a while.

# 2. Take Baby Steps

The concept of networking, or building your network, can seem daunting when looked at as a "big picture." However, when you break a project or objective into smaller pieces, you can approach it bit by bit. It's like the old adage, "How do you eat an elephant? One bite at a time." Or the advice of an ancient Chinese proverb: "The journey of a thousand miles begins but with a step." If eating an elephant or taking a journey of a thousand miles seems like a daunting task (even the first bite or the first step), you can understand why people who don't network don't like elephant meat and don't travel much.

Standing in the doorway, a networking event can seem scary. So take it step by step. Start by smiling. When you enter a room, whether you are aware of it or not, you are being observed and judged.

People make "snap judgments." Humans have done it for thousands of years, and it is part of our evolutionary development; therefore, please, no moral judgments—just acceptance of the practice. In less than a second, people will form what amounts to a full profile of you. They will create a lasting impression of your intelligence, worldview, and likeability, along with a wide range of other characteristics. Don't worry—you do the same thing. We all do it.

It's up to you to make this initial image as strong as possible, and you can do it with an opening smile—the strongest, most positive nonverbal message known to human beings. If you don't smile, the initial impression you convey will almost always be neutral to negative, and then you've started with an unnecessary hill to climb. So make it as easy on yourself as possible: *Smile!*

Establish eye contact with people in the room. You've heard the old saying, "The eyes are the windows to the soul." Well, the eyes are also the door to a conversation. You can tell whether someone is receptive to a conversation just by glancing into his or her eyes. We can't explain the analytical and clinical reasons behind this phenomenon here, but try looking into another person's eyes, and you will soon find that it works. You will recognize the person's level of receptiveness when you see it.

When you meet someone—whether you just go up and introduce yourself, someone introduces him- or herself to you, or a third party makes the introduction—repeat the name of the person you've just met or associate it with a name or person you know. For example, if you meet someone named Michelle, you can immediately associate the name with the First Lady. I'm certain this technique works because I've utilized it often. This will help you remember the name.

Next, to help get the conversation going, you can ask an open-ended question. As discussed in Chapter 2, "How to Network Effectively," an open-ended question is one for which the response cannot likely be a short one- or two-word answer (definitely not a yes/no question). Socrates was a master at this kind of question. He asked questions of people because he truly was interested in assisting them.

Open-ended questions help you surrender control of the moment. Open-ended questions don't just give the other person a choice of responses; they really allow the person to tell us what is going on in his or her mind.

Open-ended questions have these characteristics:

1. Surrender control of the conversation (or confirm the other person's control)

2. Tend to lead to longer responses, which give you more information about the other person's interests and feelings

3. Often include answers involving emotions that you can feed back

### 3. Begin with a Compliment

This is a wonderful way to start a conversation. Everyone loves to be complimented on something. Find something sincere to compliment people on anytime you have an opening to start a conversation.

### 4. Use a Script

If calling to follow up on a new contact makes you a bit nervous, develop a short yet detailed script to use. Write the key points and rehearse the script until it comes across naturally. Besides your script, have notes to refer to about the person you're calling. After you do this a few times, it may become second nature to you, and you can get by with just your notes. Using a script is a good way to develop confidence.

It's also a good idea to keep a mirror in front of your phone so that you can make sure you're smiling while you're talking. Remember the benefit of the smile? The other person knows whether you're smiling.

### 5. Work on Your Eye Contact

Recognize that not making eye contact is a disastrous mistake. Not only does it give the impression that you're not listening or paying attention, but the person with whom you're speaking might consider you rude. Even worse, avoiding eye contact can be interpreted as a sign that you have something to hide.

Andrea worked with a skilled executive named Griff who was a thoughtful and caring person. However, his colleagues and employees were concerned that he wasn't listening to them or wasn't giving them his full attention because when they spoke to him, he looked off to the side. Andrea confronted Griff with this information, and Griff told her he was shy and felt uncomfortable looking people directly in the eye. This feeling is common for shy or introverted people, but the results of not looking people in the eye are devastating for establishing relationships.

Because establishing direct eye contact was so awkward for Griff, Andrea suggested a technique called the "third eye approach," which involves looking at a spot just above and between the other person's eyes. Over time, Griff became more comfortable looking people directly in the eye. The results were amazing. People warmed up to him, his confidence grew, and his network expanded.

## 6. Attend Events and More Events

You can learn only by doing. Just reading this book alone will not make you a better networker; you have to get out and attend events where there are people to meet. Naturally, you will be inclined to start at your workplace and attend social functions. This is okay for a start, and it's also okay to continue as a regular practice, but you need to spread your wings and attend many other functions. Every community and many regional organizations hold regular functions for networking.

Sources include the local Chamber of Commerce, the Better Business Bureau, community development groups, business development and economic development organizations, sales and marketing clubs, speaker clubs—the list goes on and on. The local papers list these events, as do the websites of the various black organizations. However, don't limit yourself to only black organizations; make them a part of your diverse networking arena. Many groups sponsor breakfast, lunch, and dinner meetings, as well as cocktail receptions and other social events where people gather for the express purpose of networking.

You have to find these events and attend. African Americans who attend and network these events have a distinct advantage over their peers and classmates who do not. The reason is simple. The business decision makers, employers, and deal makers attend these events, and the African Americans who meet and network with these influencers will be remembered when opportunities arise. African Americans who do not network simply will not be in the mix and will have to get in line with the hundreds of other sheep.

## 7. Attend Events with a Purpose

Instead of going to meetings and events with just the general purpose of networking, attend only those events where you have a specific purpose in mind.

A friend of Andrea told her that he once attended an industry event for the sole purpose of meeting the speaker. The speaker was a prominent leader in the field, and Andrea's friend was writing a book related to this field and wanted to be able to send it to the speaker for an endorsement when it was finished. Therefore, the friend's objective at this event was to introduce himself to the speaker and establish a reason for a follow-up contact. He didn't care about anything else at this meeting. If he met others, that was a bonus; if the food was good, that was a bonus, too. But neither interested him. His objective was clear—and he accomplished it.

## 8. Set Up One-on-One Meetings

The next time you go to a networking event (or to any event), make it a networking opportunity. Give yourself an objective to connect with just one person and set up a follow-up, one-on-one meeting. Make this meeting at a comfortable place and at a time when you both can relax and get to know one another. Coffee shops are good venues; no one will rush you, and many have comfortable seating arrangements conducive to conversations. Getting to know someone in this atmosphere is much easier than at events and other get-togethers.

## 9. Do Your Networking at Your Highest Energy Level Time of Day

We all have a time of day when we feel more energized, when our circadian rhythms are peaking. If possible, set up meetings, make phone calls, attend events, and even do your follow-up emails and thank you notes during these high-energy times. This might not be possible if you have to attend an evening meeting and you're a morning person, but you can still deal with it. Pace yourself during the day (or even take a quick "power nap") to conserve your energy for later when you need it. The important thing is to know your own cycles and prepare ahead of time.

### 10. Set a Time Limit

One "quiet networker" Andrea knows gave this advice on dealing with networking events: Set a time limit and say to yourself, "I'll go to the meeting for one hour, and then I will go back and relax." She feels she can successfully gather her energy for an hour, whereas a full evening would be overwhelming. By using this strategy (small baby steps), she gets herself to the meetings knowing it's "only for an hour." Use this tactic in making calls. Decide how much time you will give to the task and stick to it. Don't be unrealistic; start small and remember to take baby steps. When you achieve your objective, you will be energized to continue or to go longer the next time.

### 11. Recharge and Reward Yourself

Plan a schedule so that you have time to recharge and reward yourself. This is particularly important if you are working full or part time and are going to school. You're not invincible, and you need to recharge your batteries from time to time. So do something nice for yourself. Reward yourself for accomplishing each objective you set and for achieving each "baby step" along the way. You deserve a reward, even if it's as small as reaching around and patting yourself on the back.

## Networking on the Internet

Online social networking is an efficient way to establish and maintain relationships with others in your field. Finding and meeting people on social networking sites can help you with contacts that can then aid with job searches, sales leads, and other business contacts.

Online social networking communities vary by their purpose and demographics, but the digital technologies of LinkedIn, Facebook, MySpace, Twitter, hi5, Friendster, flickr, orkut, Bebo, Ning, Doostang, and Tagged (along with other types of Web 2.0 technologies, such as wiki sites, RSS, and blogs) can create collaboration capabilities spanning time and distance barriers. Online technologies are a tool for networking. Some reports have cited that as many as 60 percent of Americans are online applying digital technology for social networking. (See Chapter 12, "Social Media: Focus on Strategy to Support Your Personal Networking," for more information on this.)

No one can deny the great efficiency of digital technologies for social contacts, but the major drawback is the lack of face-to-face contact. No amount of digital contacts can replace the high value of a face-to-face approach. Too many people use the social networking sites in a ubiquitous, incessant, compulsive drive to make dozens to hundreds of micro-digital touches that are passed off as social networking. Real networking begins and has a foundation in face-to-face encounters. Digital social networking should be viewed as a support and supplement to face-to-face networking. The daily (and sometimes hourly or more frequent) check-in or shout-out contacts are a form of social contact that's different from networking and should be viewed and treated differently.

Unquestionably, some people gain some traditional networking benefits from the micro-contact approach, but the personal ties are weak. If they're not reinforced by face-to-face encounters, no long-term trust or reciprocity will be established.

The autonomy of the Internet also makes it easier for introverts to make new connections, especially with the capabilities of online sites to create "special interest" communities. No one can see how nervous you are or notice you standing off in the corner. You can contact almost anyone you want to meet through email, and it's easier and faster than playing phone tag. Furthermore, you don't have to create a script or practice before calling. Just be sure to create an email message that states your purpose clearly and succinctly.

Still another advantage to online networking is the opportunity for you to become a known entity in your field. No fear of public speaking need deter you in this effort. You can post an article you've written, contribute to a professional website, comment on a blog, and even create your own website or blog to promote yourself and your business.

Michael's daughter, Michelle Lunsford, is, by her own admission, "quite shy and not a public person." Yet she has started a politically oriented blog on which she engages other people with whom she otherwise would have never spoken.

It seems that online networking is perfect for introverts, next-generation types, and other quiet networkers. It has advantages for sure, but introverts have to watch out for the disadvantages and problems as well.

Don't kid yourself—online networking can be just as hard work as traditional networking. You've got technical issues to deal with, as well as acceptance and privacy concerns. The Internet space is not glitch free, so those problems arise all the time. Then because of the volume of email and the fear of virus infection, spam, and pure junk email, many people filter their emails or avoid mail from senders they don't know, or they delete unopened email when the subject line is questionable, dull, or meaningless.

Lastly, online networking is just a tool of networking and should never be considered a replacement for face-to-face contacts. Your primary networking should always be face-to-face contact, with the Internet, email, postal mail, the telephone, and other communication modes as support channels.

The difference and advantage of face-to-face-networking, especially within membership-based clubs, affiliations, societies, and organizations, is apparent in the way these networked members continue to exert a powerful influence on business, education, politics, entertainment, science, economics, culture, and society in general. The obvious benefit of joining and participating in face-to-face networking with individuals in these kinds of organizations is that the networking is based on personal friendships, and people are far more willing to help friends in navigating not only these organizations, but also the areas of the culture in which they have great influence. True, the digital social sites are much larger, but they are also much less influenced by personal friendships, connections, trust, reciprocity, and rapport.

Digital networks are weaker links, but they do extend further, even across industry and geographic boundaries, which helps people link up by skill level and talent needs. They also encourage the spread of new ideas at a very rapid pace. The best characteristic of digital social networks is that they are completely inclusive, unlike some of the more traditional face-to-face organizations. Digital networks welcome anyone. However, this benefit also becomes a weakness.

For better or worse, the traditional face-to-face networking encountered through a membership-based organization is generally small enough to create a strong network because most members know each other, thus encouraging favors that will certainly be returned. Digital networks, in contrast, convey a much less loyal connection and, therefore, would not likely create the environment for as many favors.

People build trusting relationships with others by looking them in the eye, shaking their hand, and getting that "intuitive feeling" about them. As fast and efficient as the Internet is, there's still no substitute for face-to-face contact. With all the time, distance, and technological advantages of online networking, one downside has yet to be overcome: You cannot build rapport and trust online.

This chemistry is still done eye to eye in the physical presence of another person. Although we encourage the use of technological tools, they are still just tools to support what you must do primarily in person.

## Summary

When networking doesn't come easily, you might develop negative ideas about what it is and your ability to do it. Networking is about creating long-lasting relationships that are mutually beneficial. Anybody and everybody can do it; there is no "correct" way to network. Introverted or quiet people are effective networkers when they build upon their particular skill set. Develop and follow a process that fits your personality and comfort level, and you will be successful.

Think of the process as something you can *POST* on your bulletin board or on a mirror as a constant reminder:

P   Create a **plan** that fits your **personality**

O   Own it in an **organized** fashion

S   Stick to your own **system**

T   Take **time** to build relationships

Now you have the networking techniques, know the types of people you want to reach for your network, and can develop the characteristics of a good networker.

In the next chapter, you look at how to expand your network. Think of your network as your own ever-evolving "www" of contacts and resources that you can access for information and links to others. You must first build your network of websites. Next, you must learn to get the most out of this network. Finally, you need to keep your web growing, adding new contacts as some drop away and making sure you nurture all the contacts you have worked so hard to make in the first place.

# 7

# How to Expand Your Network

In this chapter, you examine tips on how to build and expand the network you currently have (that's right, you have a current network). It's all about getting the numbers, as you will see. In Chapter 8, "Keeping Your Network Alive and Growing," we talk about how to manage and develop the contacts in your network in the most efficient and effective way for you.

First, recognize that you have a network. It includes the people you know and those with whom you already have a relationship. You need to incorporate these people into five action steps that will grow and develop your network on an ongoing basis.

## The Five Action Steps of Building and Growing Your Network

Building your network takes time, patience, and an action plan. Look at the following action steps and start your process.

1. Identify the people who can help you.

2. Compare this list to a list of people you know who will take your call (see Chapter 4, "Creating Connections: The People You Will Need in Your Network").

3. Reconnect with those already in your network, and keep it up as your network grows.

4. Identify the organizations and activities where people you want to know gather.

5. Get involved in these organizations.

## *1. Identify the People Who Can Help You*

These can be specific individuals or titles of individuals within an organization, including your workplace. If you don't already know the name of the person who currently holds a particular position, find out. Always aim high. The worst that can happen is nothing. The best that can happen is that the person in the high position personally introduces you to the right contact. Of course, in the real world, neither extreme happens as often as something in between, but even something in between is far, far better than doing nothing and getting no help and no contact.

Getting the name of a contact is of vital importance in the interview process, especially if you're going in cold without the help of a network contact. We cannot stress this point strongly enough. But we can say with certainty that dozens, if not hundreds, of your peers (competitors for the jobs you want) will be arriving at the door of the company or organization for which you want to work without a name, title, or contact.

They will have their freshly printed resumes (usually poorly done) ready to hand to some human resources underling (usually not much older than themselves). Like sheep preparing for a shearing, they will be herded into cubicles for 20-minute courtesy interviews and told, "We'll be in touch if we have anything for you." If you're armed with a name and title and have set up an interview in advance, you bypass the humiliation of the shearing and useless human resources screening-out process.

You've shown initiative, leadership, courage, foresight, problem solving, and management skills, among other skills, and you are far ahead of your peers and competitors who are circling about looking for their next disappointment. Even if you don't get a job offer, you've made important steps in developing your networking, confidence building, and interviewing skills.

Furthermore, there's a chance that the manager you just met with could turn out to be a network contact. If the job interview doesn't pan out, you have a perfect opportunity, depending on the person's body language and how much of a personal connection you made, to ask the person for the names of one or two other contacts he or she could recommend for you to contact based upon your skills, abilities, and background. You might also be able to follow up with the interviewer at some point and turn him or her into a networking contact.

Don't discriminate by who can help you, how they can help, why they can help, or what they can do for you. Look at networking as a reverse-paranoid would see it: like the whole world is out to do you good!

## 2. Compare This List to a List of People You Know Will Take Your Call

Go back to the list of people who could possibly be in your network (discussed in Chapter 4). Remember, these people would take your call or return it if you called today. How many of these people are already in your network? How many might be "six degrees of separation" (or less) away from those who can help you? We think you'll find that some people already in your network have good connections you can ask for assistance.

Andrea's friend Jeri knows "everyone." She's a board member of a number of organizations, an active member of her church, and a successful professional businessperson. She attributes her success to being an active networker herself and to helping others make connections that benefit their careers. She helped Andrea by introducing her to a magazine editor Andrea had identified as someone she wanted to meet. True, Andrea could have called herself and might have gotten through eventually, but her associate, Jeri, made it possible faster and with a more personal touch. Are there more Jeris on your list?

Take another look at the individuals you know—supervisors, managers, bosses, coworkers, and members of organizations to which you belong. Have you stayed in touch? Would a note or phone call be appropriate?

What about the alumni of your college? These types of organizations often provide Andrea and me with opportunities to develop business in new industries, valuable new contacts who can help us in our professions and offer leads for business. Don't forget your neighbors and people who work in your neighborhood. In many cases, these people have seen you grow and develop and would be naturals to add to your support network. For example, think about the local coffee shop personnel, the cleaners, the lawn service, the plumber—anyone and everyone you and your family have done business with over the years.

## 3. Reconnect with Those Already in Your Network, and Keep It Up As Your Network Grows

Make a game plan of reconnecting with people already in your network who can help you. Here's an opportunity to reach out. "For what reason?" you ask. No reason. Just touch base. Say hello. Catch up on what has been happening.

And start or restart the networking connection that will be a lifeline perhaps for both of you. Don't be shy; people love calls from friends they haven't heard from in a while, especially if you don't want anything other than to say hello. Imagine the surprise of many old friends who realize the call isn't to ask for anything, but just to say hi.

Here's a game plan you can try. Consider it your FOUR-mula for success. It involves calling and connecting with four people per week from your list:

1. A person you used to work for or do business with but haven't been in touch with for a while

2. A person you used to work with

3. A friend you haven't seen or spoken to in a while

4. A current friend

Obviously, the fourth call, to a current friend, will be the easiest and the most fun. It will be your reward for making the other three calls. Work through the list by category. Create a list of people so you have plenty of names in case you come across some numbers that are no longer in service. Keep working from top to bottom, moving to the next type of call only when you've completed the previous call. Working the telephone involves a rhythm.

Set aside a block of time in a quiet space and dedicate yourself to the task of making the calls only (no disturbances and no multitasking). Keep moving through your calling list until you have completed the entire list.

It will be relatively easy to fit four completed calls a week into your busy schedule. It breaks down the formidable task of reconnecting with your list into manageable baby steps. Make this a practice you continue to use as your network grows. Most important will be the results. Imagine how easy it will be to ask for a favor now that you have solidified your relationships with so many people.

## 4. Identify the Organizations and Activities Where People You Want to Know Gather

Think of the places, associations, organizations, trade associations, clubs, conferences, events, activities, and other gatherings where people you want to meet gather. Remember the old saying, "If you want blueberries, go to where the blueberries grow." If you're interested in working in a certain field, you want to select events and activities where people will be gathered to exchange information, make contacts, gain more knowledge, or just enjoy the company of others with the same interests.

Make a list. What do you already know about these organizations? Do you belong or know anyone who belongs? Have you ever attended, or do you know anyone who has ever attended a meeting? Have you ever read any of the organization's literature? Have you been to the organization's website?

The following is a short course on how to identify and locate groups and formats that offer networking opportunities.

## Types of Networking Groups

Basically, there are four types of networking groups, categorized by purpose:

1. General networking groups

2. Industry-specific groups

3. Service groups

4. Special interest groups

Each category has different venues, different networking opportunities, and different values for the individuals attending. You must research the organization and venue, and have an idea of what type of person you expect to meet so you can prepare for the opportunity.

### General Networking Groups

These groups' stated purpose is to create networking opportunities and allow individuals to exchange leads, contacts, and tips. For the most part, these groups are for general networking and are not industry specific. The number of attendees is generally not limited.

Some of the better-known groups include these:

- Business Network International (BNI), www.bni.com

- Leads Club, www.leadsclub.com

- LeTip International, www.letip.com

- National Association for Female Executives (NAFE), www.nafe.com

- Many local chambers of commerce

These groups generally have regularly scheduled gatherings, usually monthly. The gatherings are not called meetings because there's no official agenda other than networking. The gatherings are frequently held at the same location. It's important to realize that the process is called networking, not "net–sitting around" or "net–eating and drinking" or "net–dating." The key word is *work*. And as another old saying puts it, "To the victor go the spoils."

A variant of the general networking group is the "strong" or "limited" networking group. These groups generally meet more frequently, up to four times a month, and limit the number of participants from any industry segment to one or two. The meetings are usually more structured, with every participant getting the opportunity to make a brief personal or business presentation. You might not normally get the chance to attend the strong or limited group events, but if the opportunity arises, jump at the chance.

An example of how the strong networking groups work is Business Network International (BNI), a national organization with chapters in most major U.S. cities. Each chapter has from 10 to 30 members, each from different professions, fields, or industries. Each chapter can have only one member from any given field or industry—for example, one accountant, one real estate salesperson, one stockbroker, and so on. Meetings are typically held early in the morning before the business day begins and last for about an hour. Members get 30 seconds to mention their business and describe the type of clients they hope to find. The idea is that members in the group will become familiar enough with each other's business model that they will refer clients.

At each meeting, members report the referrals they've made for their colleagues. The purpose of this organization is to network and help each other. People who belong to these groups and work hard at helping others get lots of referrals and who make lots of beneficial contacts report that they also receive many referrals and beneficial contacts. As with anything else in networking, you get what you give.

### Industry-Specific Groups

These organizations and groups are created around a specific industry or profession. Business trade associations (sometimes several) exist for every major industry group. Some subindustry groups have their own associations. Just about every profession and field has a society or trade group.

The purpose of these organizations is to represent the interests of their particular group in whatever way they can. Some organizations are quite large, active, and powerful, such as the American Association of Advertising Agencies (AAAA), Association of National Advertisers (ANA), Trial Lawyers Association, International Brotherhood of Teamsters, Boy Scouts of America, American Association of Retired Persons (AARP), and American Society of Association Executives (ASAE). These organizations have staffs numbering in the hundreds and annual budgets in excess of $100,000,000.

Networking is not always a major cause supported by these organizations. Nevertheless, the programs the associations do promote, such as educational seminars, conferences, workshops, trade shows, exhibits, panels, and other meetings, are ideal places to network with the industry leaders of the field or industry in which you want to work. Most of the events and activities these associations sponsor are open to nonmembers, and most have social activities attached to them, such as dinners, cocktail hours, breakfasts, pre-meeting get-togethers, and many other opportunities to network.

You can find any trade association by looking at the *Encyclopedia of Associations*. Your college or local library should have a copy. The encyclopedia offers an alphabetized listing of categories and an index. Another search approach is to Google the industry, field, or profession and add the search term "association." Joining and participating in the appropriate trade association for the field or industry you are interested in puts you light years ahead of your peers and competition.

After all, you will be networking with the very people who will be making the hiring decisions. They will remember and get to know you, which means a boost to your job hunting early in your career. And this, of course, gives you an advantage over your peers who do not engage in this type of networking.

## Service Groups

Many public, private, and charitable organizations with members from various walks of life exist to provide public, humane, and social services to others in need. Examples of some of these types of organizations include the following:

- Rotary International
- Lions Clubs International
- The Benevolent and Protective Order of Elks
- Kiwanis International
- Shriners International
- League of Women Voters
- Women's clubs
- Men's clubs
- Political clubs
- Student and university clubs

- Gaming clubs

- Church groups

- Parent–teacher associations

- Food pantries

- Shelters for the homeless

- Volunteer organizations

- Veteran assistance clubs

- Veterans' organizations

Whether you belong to any of these groups and use them as a networking venue depends on your individual interests and beliefs and how you use your private time. These groups exist to serve the social, community, and civic needs first, not to promote networking. However, the kind of people who volunteer and support these organizations are special. Many business and civic leaders donate their time and resources to these causes and take notice of the volunteers who work for these organizations. If you are like-minded and will benefit by meeting industry and civic leaders who might take notice of your activities, all the better. But you'd better make a real commitment and do the work for the right reasons.

Be sure to include any and all work that you do for these types of groups in the "Experience" section of your resume. Employers are looking for achievements, success in work and assignments, and leadership roles; whether you were paid for that kind of experience doesn't matter.

### Special Interest Groups

These are the groups most often overlooked in networking opportunities, yet they can be the most profitable if you keep your eyes and ears open. They are the fun groups and events: the health club, gym, book club, chess club, gaming club, gourmet cooking class, martial arts class, three-on-three basketball, and any other social get-together. How do you make connections when the activity is fun? Keep in mind that when you're doing things you like, other people are doing those things because they like to do them, too; therefore, you already have something in common. You can join, have fun, and get some networking in at the same time.

## 5. Get Involved

The following steps help you grow your network through involvement with organizations where people you want to know gather. The first three steps are particularly important and are discussed separately.

1. Go to their meetings and meet the people, then join the organizations that are best for you.

2. Volunteer, join a committee, become active, and go to the group's social events.

3. Write an article, give a speech or presentation, and do things that get you better known within the group.

4. Sign up for an RSS feed to the group's websites or other digital publications. This provides you with an ongoing feed of their thought leadership and visionary ideas.

5. Read their blogs and comment.

6. Start to IM individuals from the organization.

7. Post your own digital content to the organization's website.

8. Post your editorials, points of view (POVs), and thoughts on sites such as blip.tv, YouTube or other video upload sites, or on Twitter.

9. Add content to a wiki site related to the organization's interests.

As you will discover when researching the groups mentioned earlier, a lot of organizations and activities offer profitable networking. The trick is to find the ones best for you.

Most organizations encourage prospective members to attend a couple meetings before joining. We highly recommend this, too. No matter what you think you already know about an organization, you don't really know it until you've attended and met the members. Use your networking techniques and set a goal to meet at least two new people at each meeting you attend for each prospective organization you are considering joining. Then set a follow-up meeting with each of the people you met to get to know them better and find out more about the organization.

Be sure to ask whether the meetings you attended are typical of most meetings. Find out who generally attends meetings. Sometimes the roster of an organization includes some of the people you would like to meet, but they never attend meetings. Sometimes the meetings are the wrong environment for you to achieve your objectives in your limited time. It's important to pick organizations that are best for your needs.

You might want to consider the 2-2-2 strategy: Attend two meetings. Meet two people and exchange two business cards. Arrange for two follow-up meetings. This strategy will help you find out whether you want to join the organization and will also expand your network by at least two people. Another approach to take with an organization you are considering joining is to ask to see a list of past and future programs. Examine these for content and speakers. This information will tell you whether the organization is of interest to you. Are the speakers people you want to hear and meet? Are other programs, activities, and workshops offered that would be of interest and/or help to you? Does the organization offer a newsletter? A website? Job postings?

Is there some way you can contribute? Is the organization network friendly? Can you benefit as well as share?

## Volunteer, Join a Committee, Become Active

Michael spent 20 years in nonprofit membership organizations primarily in membership marketing. During that time, he conducted many membership satisfaction studies and gathered the results of dozens of other studies. All that data had a common and repeating theme: Active participating members get more benefit from membership organizations than members who are not active. Furthermore, they don't just get a little more benefit—they get significantly more benefit.

In many cases, they report getting returns on their investments in multiples of the money and time they spent. As a side benefit from volunteering, over and above the intrinsic feelings of reward for helping others, you can add the volunteer experience to your resume. Employers sometimes view volunteer experience and the applicant's experience and achievements with great interest. It demonstrates initiative, drive, concern for others, teamwork, leadership, organizational skills, motivation, and other soft skills that are in high demand in the workforce.

We've said it before and will say it again: Networking is hard work, but it pays off. If you network, you will be significantly ahead of your friends who do not network, in terms of career and social capital. When you become involved, you meet more people, make more contacts, get to know the organization better, and expand your network faster. Here are some ways to do this:

- **Volunteer to be a greeter.** When people are registering for a meeting or event, a greeter welcomes them. Working as a greeter is a great way to meet a lot of people. The greeter meets everyone who attends, so you will be sure to have introduced yourself to everyone attending, including those whom you wanted to meet. You will then have an "opening line" to connect with them the next time you meet.

- **Join a committee.** If you just attend meetings, you limit your ability to meet and get to know members of the organization. After all, the majority of the time spent at a meeting is devoted to the agenda and program content. Your objective is to expand your network, not just listen to a speaker—even a great one. If you volunteer for a committee or a project that interests you, you will be introduced to a number of other people.

  One of the most interesting and profitable committees to volunteer for in an organization is the program committee. As an active member of this committee, you usually get to meet and interact with all the speakers and thought leaders in the field, as well as the other committee members and most likely the organizational officers and directors.

- **Write an article, give a speech, and become known.** Remember, before you joined, you checked out the organization's roster, newsletter, list of programs, and website, and you thought about whether you could make a contribution. Now that you've had a chance to learn about the type of articles that are published in the newsletter or on the website, it's time to make a contribution. Write an article and submit it to the editor or webmaster. Even if you volunteer to write a recap of a recent meeting, you will get a byline and a publishing credit. You will become known. It will be easier to meet people when they remember you wrote an article (or you can remind them that you wrote an article). In either case, you will have made a contribution to the organization.

Another way to become known and, therefore, meet people is to give a speech or presentation for an organization. Groups are always looking for programs and breakout sessions for larger meetings or conventions. Take the opportunity to become a presenter. If you are fearful of public speaking, take a course in presentation skills; sharpen and practice these skills, because they are critical to your career success. A presentation can be as simple as teaching a basic class in a topic you know a lot about.

## Summary

To expand your network, you must create the opportunities to keep it growing and identify the people you want to meet and know. Examine your existing network and reconnect with those you've been out of touch with. Then keep it up. It's as simple as making four phone calls a week.

Look for the places you're likely to find the people you want to meet. Research and join organizations where they might gather. Don't limit yourself just to networking groups and industry organizations; think about community service and special interest groups as well. Become active in these organizations, and become known.

The more people who know who you are, the more people you have the opportunity to meet. Soon you will have a large list of contacts who will not only take your phone call, but will be glad to hear from you and glad to help you. Keeping these contacts requires time, attention, and follow-up. In the next chapter, you learn how to nurture these contacts, creating connections that last a lifetime.

# 8

# Keeping Your Network Alive and Growing

When you've been at this a while, you'll conquer your fears and develop more confidence. You'll be able to walk into rooms full of strangers (networking gold mines) with a goal of meeting and following up with at least two new people, and it will work. Congratulate yourself!

You will see the stack of business cards you've collected growing, and you will be the proud owner of a large and growing database of contacts—people who will take your phone calls, return your emails, and do favors for you. Now you have to figure out how to keep it all going. How, you wonder, do you keep in touch with these contacts and nurture the relationships you've started?

In this chapter, you consider how to keep in touch with the people in your network and build long-lasting, mutually beneficial relationships. As in any relationship, the first thing you want to do is get to know the other person's interests, family, school activities, and important events. Then you want to find ways to keep in touch. This includes the important and effective thank you note. One of the most powerful ways to stay in touch is to become a resource to others.

Finally, there's the issue of how to make sure you regularly touch base with everyone in your networking database.

## Getting to Know You

Getting to know a contact gives you information you can use to stay in touch so that everyone in your network can become a contact for life.

## Find Out the Best Way to Stay in Touch

When you meet someone you want to stay in contact with, one of the first things you will want to ask is, "What's the best way for us to keep in touch?" Everyone has a preferred way to communicate. Don't assume that because your classmates use IM and email, these are their preferred methods. Some people still prefer the telephone. Even if they can't take a call, voice mail works for them. For these people, a series of voice mail messages might be perfectly suitable. Other people prefer email and are good at responding quickly, as you should be. Many younger people respond primarily by IM, not by phone. Whatever the preference, you need to know so that your communications are as efficient as possible. Record this kind of information in your contact database.

## Note Important Dates, Birthdates, and Anniversaries

Find out important dates and events, birthdates, anniversaries, and other important occasions. Knowing such details provides an opportunity to get in touch with a card, email, IM, or phone call.

Andrea always asks about birthdays—not necessarily the year (that could be problematic), but the month and day, or even the person's astrological sign. She records this information in her contact database. Then each month she sends out an appropriate birthday reminder—cards for some, emails and phone calls for others. The fact that you remember is the important thing. Anniversaries, birthdays, and special dates are opportunities for you to reconnect and be in touch. Be alert to what people mention about these dates. Some people are proud of certain anniversaries, and the fact that you remembered will help grow the relationship.

## Family, Interests, and Hobbies

Ask your network contacts about their families, interests, and hobbies. This kind of information gives you conversation starters (everyone loves to talk about themselves). It also provides you with information that helps you stay in touch. Finally, this kind of information can give you ideas that can make you a resource for other people and turn you into a strong contact for them.

# Ways to Keep in Touch and Show Appreciation

When you're armed with information, here are some ways you can use it to keep in touch and help build your relationships.

## *Use Notes*

There is something that differentiates you and sets you apart when you write someone a handwritten note. You took the time to sit down and craft a thoughtful note. The note has become something of a rarity in today's world. When you write one you will stand out and be remembered.

### Handwritten Notes

Sadly, the art of drafting handwritten notes, especially in college, is disappearing. The U.S. Postal Service reports that only 4 percent of mail is personal correspondence. However, this mode of communication is your key to success. What have you learned in your marketing and communications classes? Differentiation is how you stand out and get noticed. If you send handwritten notes, we guarantee that they'll be noticed and read. Think about it: When you open your mailbox, doesn't a handwritten envelope stand out among all the other mail, and don't you read it first? And doesn't the thought cross your mind, "Someone is thinking of me"? A personal note is the most effective way to connect and reconnect with others and make them feel good about knowing you.

### Thank You Notes

One of the very best and least expensive public relations tools you can use is the simple thank you note. As discussed in Chapter 5, "Characteristics of Great Networkers," you can never say "thank you" too many times, as long as it's sincere.

Here are eight reasons to send a thank you note:

1. For time and consideration given to you
2. For being interviewed for a job
3. For a compliment you received
4. For a piece of advice you received

5. For business you received

6. For a referral you were given

7. For a gift someone gave you

8. For help someone gave you

It makes good sense to have notecards and stamps close by so that, in your spare time, you can write a note or two and drop them in the mail. Software online also can generate note cards with your personal message in a handwriting font; thus, the note appears handwritten even though you've typed it on your computer. You simply print it, put a stamp on it, and mail it. Check Andrea's website (www.selfmarketing.com) for more information on this service, which she uses herself.

## Other Notes

Besides the thank you note, you can send several other types of notes anytime to stay in touch and be helpful.

- **FYI (for your information).** You can send articles, clippings, or URL addresses that might be of interest to people in your network. These notes can be related to the recipient's business, college courses, family, hobbies, personal interests, or something else you think he or she might be interested in. Include a brief note, such as, "I thought of you when I came across this and thought you might [enjoy it, find it useful, be interested in it, want it for your files, and so on]."

- **Congratulations.** Send one of these notes for a new job, a promotion, an award, an honor, or any event for which your network contact received recognition. This is a perfect opportunity to stay in touch.

- **Nice talking with you.** Andrea sends these notes after a phone conversation (especially a phone appointment or conference call), a meeting, and a chance encounter and conversation, and always after meeting someone new at an event.

- **Thinking of you.** These notes are sent for no particular reason other than to stay in touch. They're easy to use—you can buy a card with this sentiment and just add a brief note.

## Holiday Notes

Andrea sends holiday greetings to everyone in her network contact list and uses other occasions to remember to stay in touch as well. Think about your network contacts. Could you send Thanksgiving, Easter, St. Patrick's Day, Friendship Week, Mother's Day, or Father's Day cards? The calendar is full of special day opportunities you can use to stay in touch.

## "The Power of Three" Note Plan

You may be thinking, "That's a lot of notes and cards! Who has the time?" Here's a technique Andrea adopted and has used successfully for years. It's easy and doesn't take much time out of your busy day. Moreover, we can say from experience that you can be sure it will pay off in building solid networking relationships. Every day, send three handwritten notes. Make them short notes to express any of the messages we've discussed. You can send these notes to these people, among others:

- Fellow students
- Former coworkers
- Friends
- Family members
- Club and association members
- Former teachers
- Prospective contacts
- Customers

If you write and send just three notes a day, by the end of the workweek, you will have contacted 15 people—and by the end of the year, 750 people (assuming that you take a couple of weeks off). Try to make these handwritten notes in addition to the thank you and follow-up notes you would normally send.

Writing these notes shouldn't take more than 10 minutes a day. You can write them first thing in the morning before classes, during lunch, after your classes end, or whenever works best for your schedule. Writing notes is easy when you get into the habit. Your note doesn't have to be perfectly crafted—it's the thought that counts.

When you get the hang of this technique, add in a multiplier and a total of:

- Three extra notes
- Three extra emails
- Three extra phone calls

That's 2,250 connections in a year! Andrea uses this system and finds it great for continually staying in touch with her contacts.

## Take Full Advantage of Email

The handwritten note is a special note; however, in today's world, we are fortunate to have a way to be in instant contact with so many people all around the world. In fact, there is very little excuse for not showing appreciation or following up in a timely fashion with email. It's perfectly appropriate to send a thank you note via email for any of the eight reasons mentioned earlier. It's also fine to send an article of interest as an email attachment. Just be careful not to bombard your network contacts with articles, notes, or (shudder) chain letters that are making the rounds on the Internet. Remember, you are extending a professional courtesy, so the message should be tailored to the recipient, not a mass mailing. Make sure you have a valid reason to send the information, and always include a personal note. We talk about networking etiquette in the next chapter, but for now, remember to follow one fast rule about email correspondence: Always reply to emails within 48 hours of receipt. Not responding quickly makes you appear uninterested and even rude.

## Send Gifts

Sometimes it's appropriate to show appreciation with a gift. Sending a gift sets you apart. When is it appropriate to send a gift? Andrea often sends a gift after she completes a project, when someone gets promoted, for a birthday or holiday, or when someone has done her a special favor.

In business and academic situations, you need to be careful about the nature of the gift. Keep in mind that this is a gesture of appreciation; you don't want to place the recipient in the awkward position of having to turn down your gift due to company or school policy. In general, food is the best kind of gift in this situation. Most businesses or universities do not allow gifts to employees, but professors will allow a gift of food to be shared with all. Some good choices include a fruit basket, a popcorn tin, or a box of candy or other edible goodies.

# Follow-ups: The Key to Keeping Your Network Alive and Growing

You could be the master of working a room and leave each networking event with a pocketful of business cards, but if you don't follow up with these people and others already in your network, you will never succeed at networking. Follow-up is the key.

## *When Should You Follow Up?*

There are four absolute must-follow-up situations. When you follow up in these situations and in the time suggested, you will successfully create and maintain an active list of contacts who trust and respect you and who will gladly help you when you need it. Here are the situations and how to follow up:

1.  Within 24 hours after a meeting, send a note or email, or call by phone to say any of the following, depending on the circumstances of your meeting:

    "How nice to meet you."

    "Thank you for your time and consideration."

    "We should meet again."

    "Thank you for the useful information."

    This is not only a courtesy, but it also differentiates you from the myriad others they have met.

2.  If you promised to send materials, set up a meeting, or pass on a referral, keep your word and do it within the time promised—or sooner. It's easy to make these promises at a meeting or event,

but following up in a timely manner makes you remembered and trusted.

3. Call within two weeks of having made a suggestion to get together, whether over a meal or at a more formal meeting. Just saying "Let's do lunch" is not an effective networking technique. Don't suggest it unless you mean it, and then follow up to set a specific date and place. Twenty-four hours before your get-together, call again to confirm. When you follow up in this manner, you're perceived as sincere and professional.

4. If a contact gives you a referral or passes on your resume to help you, be sure to thank your contact and let him or her know the results. You should also do this for any tangible advice given to you from a network contact. People who offer help to you in whatever form deserve to know the results of their advice. More important, they absolutely deserve a thank you.

Following up not only shows good communication skills, but also builds solid relationships for the future and shows respect for others. It helps people remember you and makes them more willing to continue helping you.

## Become a Resource for Others

Share your skills and experience, happy in the knowledge that you are helping friends and fellow students and colleagues. Other people appreciate and seek out knowledgeable individuals who give generously of their expertise. When you've been a resource to others, people are more willing to help you when you ask.

Andrea had a client by the name of Kesha who was a good example of this. Kesha always went out of her way to help others. When people needed something, they called on Kesha. It was no surprise that when Kesha lost her job in a corporate downsizing a few years ago, she only had to make a few calls to some close network contacts, and she was back to work in no time—with a better and more prestigious position. It was easy for her to ask for help because she had consistently been so helpful to so many others.

## Face-to-Face Time

When you can spend time with someone in person, sharing that experience is always more powerful, effective, and memorable than carrying on a conversation by phone, IM, or email. The reason for this is what we call *chemistry*. Sociologists call it *rapport*, but many people just refer to it as *connecting*.

You know the feeling—the energy and excitement you feel when you've created a strong bond with someone over common interests or issues. This rapport can be formed and felt only when you are in the other person's physical presence and can look into his or her eyes. The bond of rapport can make someone a colleague, a friend, and certainly a strong network contact.

People love doing things for and with other people they know and like. This phenomenon has positive health benefits. Making network contacts actually helps strengthen a positive mental outlook for people. In today's busy world, finding the time to make face-to face contacts is increasingly difficult. Distance is also a limiting factor. However, like many other things, if you make a plan, you are much more likely to carry out the activity. So make a plan to spend some time in face-to-face contact with certain network contacts. Face-to-face meetings require more planning, so plan them at least 30 to 60 days in advance.

You have to be both persistent and creative to make sure you get this face time. Besides traditional meetings such as breakfast, lunch, dinner, and after-work outings, suggest getting together for coffee, tennis, or golf, meeting at a museum, or going to an industry or academic meeting together. Think creatively. Everybody is busy and appreciates new and unique suggestions. Be persistent; face-to-face meetings are invaluable in building solid networking relationships.

## Plan to Keep in Touch with Everyone in Your Growing Network

As your network continues to grow, you will want to have a system for staying in touch with each of your network contacts. We're frequently asked how we keep in touch with several thousand people on each of our networking lists. Here's how we do it.

Divide the list into three categories: A, B, and C. There's a contact plan for each category. The C list is made up of "touch base" people. These are casual acquaintances—interesting people we've met and with whom we want to stay in touch, and with whom we have no immediate personal involvement or business connection. Each person gets a quarterly contact of some sort. Andrea sends a quarterly newsletter. I send an "update note," or a short interesting article with a note, "Have you seen this?" Holiday cards are appropriate.

The B list is made up of "associates." We're actively involved with these people, either professionally or personally. We find ways to meet each of them in person, for a meal, coffee, tea, snack, or chat at least two times a year. In addition, we send them up to six personal notes a year. We call them every other month just to say hello. We also give these individuals holiday cards and gifts, and Andrea sends her B list her newsletter.

The A list is made up of close friends and associates. We see these individuals in person at least four times a year. We frequently give them special gifts and contact them with personal notes and calls. We send these individuals articles of interest, as well as newsletters and holiday cards.

The A, B, and C lists aren't static, and the rules aren't forged in stone. This system represents a plan and provides a road map for how to manage a contact list effectively.

## MAKE *FACE* WORK FOR YOU

F  Make it **fun**. **Find** unique things to do and places to meet.

A  **Adapt** to each other's timetable and surroundings.

C  **Connect** and find **common** interests.

E  Know when to **exit**. Be respectful of each other's time.

# Summary

In this chapter, you explored how to keep your network alive and growing. You have to nurture and tend to your network much the way a gardener tends to his or her garden. First you plant seeds, then you water and feed the growing plants, and then, hopefully, they will blossom. For your network, first you make the contact; then you follow up, become a resource, and stay in touch; and then, hopefully, you create relationships that grow and are mutually beneficial. Your network, just like a garden, will grow and prosper only if you take the time to tend to it carefully.

As in any social business discourse, rules of etiquette and conventional behavior should be observed. Sadly, in today's world, driven by short-term results, many of these rules and conventions are ignored. We call this phenomenon "negative networking." Not only is it rude—it just doesn't work. The next chapter reviews these rules of etiquette and offers some examples of how to avoid negative networking.

ST. JOHN THE BAPTIST PARISH LIBRARY
2920 NEW HIGHWAY 51
LAPLACE, LOUISIANA 70068

# 9

# Networking Etiquette

**W**hat would you think if you were at a wedding reception and a guest seated across from you began handing out business cards? At first, you might just think the person was outgoing and friendly, but what would you think if this guest then began asking everyone at the table questions about their personal investments? Worse, what if this bore began bragging about how he could do better than you were doing now, regardless of your situation?

Still worse, what if this embarrassment of a so-called networker called everyone at the table and asked for a meeting and referrals? Obviously, he's a disaster of a networker—this is an actual event that happened to Andrea. This was truly poor networking etiquette—negative networking, as we call it. Networking is all about establishing positive relationships and building trust and reciprocity. In our example, the man started working on the table before the soup was served. Not only did he not bother to get to know the people at the table, but he also showed poor manners and lack of common courtesy.

Etiquette is just plain good manners, common courtesy. Successful business relationships, just like successful personal relationships, rely on common courtesy.

In this chapter, you look at some rules of etiquette that relate to networking activities but that should be remembered and observed in *any* business or social situation. Most of us learned the basic rules of etiquette from our parents, peers, and mentors as we grew up—and sometimes by observation. A description follows of some common networking situations and rules for the proper etiquette for each.

# Networking Events, Meetings, or Activities

When you attend any type of event, there needs to be both a structure and strategy to maximize the opportunities. Follow these suggestions and see what happens.

1. Arrive on time—or, better yet, early. Showing up late shows disrespect and is a red flag of poor character. It signals that you think your time is more important and valuable than those at the meeting. Early arrival demonstrates enthusiasm and respect for people's time. Furthermore, an early arrival gives you time to settle in and further plan your activities.

2. Place your name tag on the right side and as high as appropriate on your garment. This places it in a direct line of eye contact with the people you meet and helps people see and remember your name.

3. Exchange business cards with ease. Place several loose cards in your right pocket or in a spot where you can reach them easily without digging or rummaging through your pockets, purse, or wallet. Make sure your business cards are fresh.

4. Don't walk around with a stack of resumes, and don't just hand out your resumes to everyone you meet. Keep your resumes in a folder or attaché until it becomes obvious one is needed.

5. Make eye contact with each person you're about to meet. Looking someone in the eye shows respect and indicates that you are honest and trustworthy.

6. Shake hands (if appropriate) firmly. Nothing is worse than a cold, fishy, loose grip. On the other hand, don't go for a death grip, either. This isn't a contest to prove your strength.

7. Be aware of the difference in business, social, and personal space. Business space is five or more feet apart and conveys proper business distance. Social space is between four and two feet and conveys a warmer, friendlier feeling in which you can discuss almost any topic. Personal space is closer than two feet and causes many people discomfort unless they invite you into their space by

shaking your hand with a double-grasp, pulling you in, placing a hand on your shoulder, or otherwise moving to close the space.

8. Welcome others into your conversation with grace and a smile. Extend your hand(s), welcome, and be inclusive.

9. Don't eat and carry on a conversation. Do one or the other, but not both at the same time.

10. If you drink and carry on a conversation, either use little or no ice or wrap napkins around the glass. A cold glass leads to a cold handshake.

## Meals at Large Events or Private Functions

The opportunities to meet and connect at any meal or function are great networking moments. To maximize your time, take a look at the following etiquette tips.

1. Turn off your cell phone. Answering—or, worse yet, making—a call at such an event shows disrespect. It says that the people at the event aren't important.

2. First, introduce yourself to the person seated on your right and then your left. Then introduce yourself to the rest of the table. As others join the table, introduce yourself and others to them.

3. Wait for those at the head table to begin eating, or if you're at a private meal, wait for the host or hostess to begin. If you are the host or hostess, you must begin.

4. When ordering, allow your guest to order first. Direct the server first to your guest, then select your entrée accordingly. It is safest to pick something in the midprice range.

5. If you don't know which utensil to use, working from the outside in is always a safe start. Alternatively, watch the host or hostess.

6. Keep your napkin on your lap until you leave the event. If you leave the table, temporarily place the napkin on your chair. When you've finished your meal, place the napkin next to your plate.

7. Water glasses and salad plates work this way: Liquids on the right, solids on the left.

8. When you're finished, place your knife and fork in a parallel position across the center of your plate.

9. Even if you're still hungry, stop eating if everyone else at the table is done.

10. Don't talk with your mouth full. (Also, don't talk with your mind empty.)

11. Hold off talking about business until the main course is cleared. This allows ample time for making small talk and getting acquainted. In addition, the servers will be out of the way.

12. Ask before you take notes. It is perfectly acceptable to take notes at a business networking event, but first ask out of courtesy. Use a small notepad or index cards, not a full-size notebook or a laptop.

## *Making Introductions*

In the business world, when introducing two people, defer to position and age. Gender is not a factor. Try to include something that the individuals might have in common. An introduction is normally made in a logical order:

1. **Younger to older.** For example: "Mr. President, I would like to introduce my daughter, Sue, the president of her eighth-grade class."

2. **Your company peer to a peer in another company.** For example: "Darius, since we have not yet worked on projects together, this is someone I wanted you to meet and someone with whom I worked with previously on many projects, Linda Jones."

3. **Junior executive to senior executive.** For example: "Joan Roberts, Manager of Logistics, please meet our CEO Susan White, whom I believe got her start in business in logistics."

4. **Fellow executive to client.** For example: "Robert, I would like to introduce you to the Purchasing Manager of XYZ Company, Joe Smith."

5. **Personal contact to business contact.** For example: "Maria is a friend of mine, and I have wanted her to meet someone who knows as much about accounting as she does. Maria, this is Don."

## Email and IM Etiquette

Email and IM make our lives easier because they're immediate, efficient, and convenient. They're wonderful communication tools; however, sometimes your messages can be misunderstood if you don't follow certain conventions. We realize that young people have a unique language and relaxed rules for spelling and grammar online. However, keep this in mind:

Digital messages are forever. Any digital message or signal that you send stays in cyberspace forever. You can delete it from your computer, but after you send it, someplace, sometime, any message can be recalled by somebody. After you press the Send button, the message is no longer yours—it belongs to whoever has possession of it.

Also bear in mind that email and IM lack the vocal inflections required to express tone, regardless of the icons, tags, and other devices that attempt to convey emotions and feelings. You can't digitize body language—yet.

Here are some digital communications etiquette tips:

1. Keep digital communications brief, to the point, and focused.

2. Use meaningful, thoughtful subject lines.

3. Use a format: purpose, body, and action.

4. If you need to send a long document, send it as an attachment.

5. Do not forward jokes, chain letters, flame letters, or other junk email or other IMs.

6. Never email or IM when you're angry or emotional or when your judgment is clouded. Better to wait a few hours or a day.

7. Always reread your message before pressing send. Make sure you're saying what you want to say.

8. Answer all emails within 48 hours.

## Phone Etiquette

We are attached to our smartphones 24/7. There is a true art and etiquette to using the phone and being remembered as poised, professional, and prepared.

1. Return all phone calls within 48 hours, even if you don't have an answer yet. Let your caller know you're working on the issue.

2. When making a phone call, ask the person if this is a good time to talk; if not, ask when a good time is, and follow the other person's lead.

3. State the purpose of your call and indicate that you would like a few minutes of the person's time. Don't take any longer unless the other person insists.

4. When leaving a message, clearly and succinctly state your name, purpose of the call, and the action you need. Most importantly, when leaving your number, speak slowly and clearly.

5. When calling a contact referral, state your name and who referred you. For example: "Hello, my name is Michael Faulkner. Andrea Nierenberg suggested I give you a call to ask if you would be kind enough to tell me about how you have been so successful in launching a new product during this recession. Is this a good time to talk?"

6. Smile when you're talking. The other person can't see you, but he or she can tell in your voice whether you're smiling.

7. Don't multitask while on the phone. People can tell when you're trying to do several things at once. It's rude and disrespectful.

8. Don't put the other person on speakerphone unless it's absolutely unavoidable or the person requests it.

## The Right Way to Ask for a Favor

When you've been a good resource to others, it's easy to ask for a favor. Most people are happy to help, especially if you know how to ask. Here are some opening lines to use:

- "Perhaps you could help me..."

- "Who do you know that _____?"

- "Would you feel comfortable referring me to _____?"

- "I would really appreciate your help on..."

- "I'd like to get your advice on..."

- "Maybe you could steer me in the right direction."

- "If you were in my shoes, what would you do?"

- "How would you handle this?"

- "There's something I could really use your expert advice with."

- "It would be wonderful if I could get your opinion (or advice) on something. Would you consider helping me?"

Always remember to say thank you and follow up with an email, a handwritten thank you note, and a gift, if appropriate.

## Following Up

Following up is always good networking etiquette.

1. Always send a thank you note or an email within 48 hours after a meeting. Thank your contact for his or her time and consideration, and confirm any follow-up steps.

2. Get permission for any "next steps." Ask when would be a good time to call or get together. Also ask, "What is the best way for us to keep in touch?" The person may prefer IM, email, telephone, letter, or a face-to-face meeting. These steps show respect for the other person's time and preference.

3. Be sure to follow up when asked specific questions. When asked specifically for a referral, materials, data, your resume, or other source material or information, ask, "When do you need this?" And then send it on time—or earlier.

# Networking at a Non-Networking Event

If you think of networking as connecting, learning about and helping others, and building relationships, then you can see that it can be done anywhere, anytime.

However, remember how inappropriately the stockbroker acted at the wedding? Had he been at a meeting specifically for networking, his actions might have been marginally more appropriate. The purpose of a networking meeting is to share personal information and ask for referrals.

The purpose of a wedding reception, a dinner, a party, or many other social events is to celebrate. Does this mean you shouldn't meet people at such functions or begin to establish relationships? Of course not; however, the proper way to do this at social events and other non-networking events is with discretion. Follow these rules, and you won't get into trouble:

1. Recognize where you are, the purpose of the event, and why you are there.

2. When you come across a potential network contact, graciously suggest that perhaps this isn't the best time to discuss business/networking opportunities and suggest a call for a later date. Offer some options. This is a perfect example of why you need business cards.

3. Ask permission before exchanging business cards or personal information. Then the exchange should be as discreet as handing a tip to a maître d'.

4. Recognize that conducting business is simply not allowed at several types of establishments, such as private clubs, where conducting business is simply not allowed. Be aware of where you are, and follow the prescribed behavior.

# Keeping Score

For some people, networking means that they do someone a favor, and a favor is owed to them in return. It's almost as if they keep a scorecard for every contact. Andrea and Renee just believe in helping others, and if they receive something in return, they consider it a gift, not a right or a privilege. Here are some guidelines on "keeping score":

1. Always return a favor given to you.

2. Don't expect or demand that a favor be returned to you.

3. Give only for the sake of giving.

4. Underpromise and overdeliver.

## Networking Competition

We would like to make another point about competition and networking. By their nature, some people are very competitive. There's nothing inherently wrong with "keeping score" and trying to be the best networker possible, but you need to be cautious about turning your networking into a competition just to win or to build up the largest number of contacts or to be the first in your graduating class to get a job or a promotion using networking. Networking is a professional experience. Using it to keep pace with your classmates or to rack up numbers of contacts, or solely as a means to an end, is a misuse of networking's purpose.

## Summary

This chapter stressed the importance of etiquette in networking. It is important to recognize that networking and good manners are compatible. Networking is about building relationships with others, and as in any relationship, common courtesy counts.

Are you wondering how to keep track of all the contacts and information you're gathering as you master the networking process? In the next chapter, you consider how to organize and keep track of thousands of contacts.

# 10

# Organizing and Keeping Track of Your Network

D on't expect this chapter to be full of high-tech jargon and recommendations for state-of-the-art computer hardware and software. Our theory is that you should use the KISS system, or you won't keep any system at all. What's the KISS system? Keep It Simple, Stupid (said lovingly, of course). Any system you want to use will work, whether you use index cards, sticky notes, or a database system such as ACT!, Excel, Lotus Notes, or GoldMine. Whatever system you use, it needs to be easy to use and simple to access, or you will not use it consistently. Your system should work for you; you should not have to work for your system. The master networkers live by this saying. They always have the information they need at hand because their system is organized and accessible. Take time to set up a system, and then be sure to keep it up-to-date.

## Setting Up a Networking Database

Organizing your database of contacts will keep your universal network growing and you will be able to manage it with ease and finesse.

1. First enter the basic contact information: name, title, company/ school, address, phone number (cell, land line), fax number, email address, URL (if appropriate), and BlackBerry number.

2. Enter each contact's preferred method of communication.

3. Enter any details you want to remember, such as personal interests, favorite books, clubs they've joined, sports they enjoy or play, food they like, their majors in school, hobbies and interests, arts and entertainment interests, favorite music and bands,

family information, organizations to which they belong, job information, and birthday and holiday information.

4. Use A, B, C prioritizing (see Chapter 8, "Keeping Your Network Alive and Growing").

5. Make notes on your history of contacts and conversations.

6. Enter the best time and place to contact this person.

## Summary

No matter how you choose to organize your database of network contacts and information, you need to devise a system and stick to it. A key to successful networking is follow up. Having a well-organized and up-to-date database, and a system for accessing it, will help you do this.

In Chapter 11, "Tying It All Together," you look at the plans, commitments, and successes of some people like you who have used nonstop networking techniques to achieve their goals and dreams in life.

# 11

# Tying It All Together

W e're always delighted when we get an IM, or the phone rings, or we get an email and a contact informs us that we were right, these techniques really do work, and the person wants to share his or her story with us. We hear stories all the time about new job offers, exciting new career opportunities, fantastic business ventures, wonderful new relationships, or just accounts of newfound confidence or personal development in meeting people and making connections. The letters and messages we receive in which people say that their lives have been transformed because they made networking a part of their daily existence are the most gratifying of all.

We hope that you, too, are benefiting, or will benefit, from the principles, tools, rules, ideas, and techniques of nonstop networking. You can incorporate every single thing we've talked about in each chapter—from attitude and techniques to continuity and organization—into your daily life starting *now*.

- **Attitude:** Networking is a lifelong process.

- **Techniques:** You have all the techniques at hand to make it happen.

- **People:** Every contact you make is the chance to learn something new.

- **Organization:** Keeping contacts and information at your fingertips is easy and rewarding.

# Attitude Is Everything

When you started this journey, you saw how a negative attitude could stop you from networking—how negative attitudes actually *do* stop people from networking.

This was the case with the students in the UCLA survey, who, by an overwhelming margin, saw that networking was successful but couldn't bring themselves to do what it took to succeed. Yet when you give yourself permission to network and change from a negative to a positive outlook, good things begin to happen. Your success really is in your hands and mind.

You'll find a common theme among these and other stories of successful networkers: The harder they work, the luckier they seem to be. Go figure. (The names and some details in the following stories have been changed to protect the privacy of all parties involved.)

# The Photographer's Story

Andrea's friend Judy, a photographer, asked, "What do you mean, 'The opposite of networking is 'not working'?" That didn't make sense to her. It seemed to her that networking is not only work, but hard work! But Andrea meant that when you're not networking, you're simply not working. You're just standing still in life, like the photographer who was afraid to get out there and network, to get clients and start her own business.

Judy followed the steps in this book: "I took baby steps. I planned what to say when I met new people. I developed a 30-second infomercial about myself. I went through my old address books and reconnected with old friends and colleagues. The more I did, the better I became at these skills. "Actually, it wasn't as though I was not good at it in the first place. I liked meeting people. It was just that I had a bad attitude about *networking.*"

What happened as a result was an epiphany of sorts, she explains: "I stopped thinking about myself and networking for my business and focused on the people I was meeting and reconnecting with. As Andrea suggested, I looked for ways to be a resource and to make connections. I love to entertain, so I put together a series of dinner parties where I concentrated on putting together people I thought would enjoy meeting one another. I also hosted a number of neighborhood get-togethers." After one such event, she remarked to her husband, "We are so fortunate to have so many interesting neighbors, from all walks of life."

Sure enough, her network expanded as she continued to meet people and reconnect with those she had lost touch with. "I was having fun!" she says. "And my business got off the ground. My 30-second infomercial was effective—I think mostly because I am so enthusiastic about my new profession. Also, everyone has something to say about photography, and almost everyone needs a portrait of themselves or a family member, a pet, or even a house."

Now Judy knows what Andrea means when she says that every single person we meet is someone we have an opportunity to learn from. "Everyone has something to offer. Who knows? That person may turn out to be a potential client for you. My business is still young, but all the clients I have so far have come from networking efforts. The amazing thing is I don't think of it as networking. It is just meeting people and talking about something I love to do."

## Armed with Your Arsenal

You have all the techniques at hand to succeed. You can use them at any event or in any situation that arises. To use them effectively, just remember the following:

- Know who you are.
- Focus on the needs of others.
- Have a goal.
- Work at it.

Know who you are. How do you want people to remember you? Is it more than just your business card? Is it a comment or remark you make that causes someone to say, "Oh really? How do you know that?" Is it the description of yourself delivered with natural enthusiasm and, yes, even passion?

Focus on the needs of others. Keep your conversation starters and "get to know you" questions fresh and timely and focused on the other person's needs.

Practice your openers and watch how your conversations become easier and more interesting. Your goal is to get others talking about themselves so that you can learn their needs and how you can be a resource to them.

Have a goal. Networking is a lifelong process; however, your networking goals will change throughout your life. At any given time, you might be more or less concerned with the following:

- Finding a job
- Getting a promotion
- Looking for a career change
- Finding a life partner
- Looking for a new business venture
- Looking for new business clients
- Examining your political aspirations
- Reevaluating your personal interests
- Looking for a lifestyle change
- Moving to a new location
- Getting interesting assignments and the best project teams

Keep working; never quit. Networking is a lifelong journey that will bring a lifetime of rewards to those who keep working at it. Armed with the techniques in this book, you can accomplish your goals in these or any areas of your life.

## Darius's Story

Darius, one of Michael's students, says the most important concept he learned in college, and the idea that Michael stressed the most in class, was the importance of networking. From reading Andrea's first book on networking and attending Michael's lectures, Darius started to take a different approach to the way he did a lot of things, especially how he presented himself when meeting people for the first time. "One major thing I have learned is the importance of understanding body language and the effect it has on networking and the perceptions of others," Darius says. "People form perceptions of you before even meeting and getting to know you."

The real test came when the college career services department put Darius in touch with a company called Berry Plastics. The firm wanted a copy of his resume. With Michael's help, Darius created an achievement-oriented resume that focused on the kind of skills and character traits businesses want in new college graduates. The initial interview led to others, and Darius built a network of contacts with each new person he met. When he was ultimately hired by Berry Plastics, several departments requested that Darius be assigned to them.

Darius attributes much of his success to changing his resume to focus on his accomplishments at past jobs. He also made sure he followed up with a handwritten thank you note to everyone who interviewed him.

Getting an internship at a large facility with more than 300 employees gave Darius the perfect venue for putting into practice his newfound networking skills. While working in different areas of the company, he met people with different levels of authority and people of different races and age groups. Before he knew it, he'd gotten to know at least 50 people and made a good impression. In the future, if he needed anything, he felt like he could ask any of them for a favor.

Along the way, Darius was careful to monitor his image. "I watched how I presented myself at all times, making sure to project good body language even if someone did something that annoyed me, such as not getting me some type of information I needed at a certain time," he says. That focus on creating a positive image with all the management in the company paid off. Whenever Darius was introduced to an auditor or someone in a higher level of authority, the person doing the introductions always said something good about him. This helped Darius meet and get to know a lot of people in respectable positions. He networked with the right people to put a positive image of himself in their minds.

This process ultimately introduced Darius to his current contact, the vice president of business and financial planning for the company. Berry

Plastics holds an annual meeting where three top people, one of whom is the vice president, come in for an all-day session to go over the financials of the company.

Throughout the meeting, a lot of management had good things to say about Darius and how he'd helped them. After hearing all this, the vice president sought out Darius and introduced himself; he then asked Darius if he was interested in staying with the company because of the great things people had said about him.

Darius is now training to get to know more about the company and to see if this is the career path he'd like to take. The company is willing to create a position for him, and the financial manager of half the company is even making a trip to spend time with him. And all this started through networking.

## Deborah's Story

Andrea's friend Deborah, a vice president of an advertising agency, found her life partner by setting a goal and using networking techniques.

First, Deborah wrote out exactly what she was looking for in a life partner. For starters, he had to be a certain age and religion, and he had to come from a background similar to her own. He had to have many of the same interests as her, including a zest for travel. Most important, Deborah wanted someone who shared her values and goals, especially about raising a family.

Next, she identified the places where she would likely meet such a person. She joined specific business and social interest groups, she got more involved in her church, and she taught a course at a local community college. She joined a board of a local nonprofit group and volunteered to chair an event. She also began networking at her health club. Deborah was just living her life, but she added a networking component.

Deborah joined and got involved with things that interested her, but with the specific goal of making contacts, knowing that one of these contacts might turn out to be, or might lead to, her life partner. She also subtly told others about her goal. In business terms, she asked for referrals. Ultimately, that's how she met Doug, whom she married a year ago.

Along the way, Deborah met many interesting people, dated several prospective life partners, made some beneficial business connections, and found some lifelong friends. She says she also fine-tuned networking techniques, which have served her well in a subsequent job search.

## Char's Story

Char and Renee met several years ago while working in the education industry. Over time, Char asked Renee to be her mentor. Being a mentor is an endeavor that Renee did not take likely. A mentor has responsibilities to the mentee; it is a mutually beneficial relationship. A mentoring relationship provides an exchange of information from both parties. When asked to take on this undertaking, Renee had to first understand her own philosophy and examine how her experiences had shaped her, the finished product. Her experiences had shaped her, and her mentee's experiences had shaped her. The challenge for her was how to inspire her to reach the goals she'd set. Renee's role was to share knowledge, expertise, and influence to develop Char's behavior, goals, and success.

Recently, Char called Renee to share the good news that she'd obtained a new position after being laid off for a few months. Char said she'd realized the importance of networking when she entered the education industry in 2005 and was introduced to the president of the school. She shared her experiences of learning work ethics, which she has carried throughout her career. She constantly does networking, whether she's working or not working. She's aware of her personal stumbling blocks and works on them to ensure that they don't impede her career progress.

During the time Char was laid off, in early 2011, a friend reached out to her and told her that the president of the school they'd used to work for was at a location in New Jersey. Fortunately, the president's administrative assistant was someone she'd worked with in 2005. Char sent an email to his assistant reintroducing herself and asking about job opportunities. The person acknowledged Char's email and forwarded her resume to a branch with an opening that matched her qualifications. The campus director immediately contacted her to set up an interview. The interviewer told Char that she came highly recommended, but her skill set was beyond the position she was interviewing for. He offered her not only another position, but an opportunity to be groomed for upward mobility. Char was hired within two hours of the interview. Each position Char previously received in education had come from networking within her strong ties; this was her first position found via weak ties.

Networking also worked for Char because she connected herself with like-minded women who seek advancement without any type of envy; this is a rarity among a group of black women. She aligned herself with a purposeful inner circle of women who are on the move and are driven by results. This was her first experience with networking succeeding outside her racial background. If African Americans aren't afraid to go outside their comfort zone and utilize those weak ties, it's possible to make networking really work.

## Identify and Expand

Every contact you meet is the chance to learn something new. Keep identifying these people and the places where they gather. Build on your current database of contacts, and seek out new ones. These contacts enrich your life and lead you to relationships that help you achieve your life's goals.

## Tom's Story

Tom, Andrea's friend and former publicist, successfully incorporated a networking plan into his business plan. This has helped him stay on track to expand his network and grow his business.

Before he opened a new office in downtown Chicago for his growing public relations firm, Tom wrote a business plan that included a networking strategy. He had been working with Andrea for a number of years, and she'd already taught him the techniques of networking. Tom also knew from firsthand observation of the growth of Andrea's business that the techniques worked. "Since a key aspect of public relations is building relationships with the media, the first thing I did was find a location close to the offices of every major national and local media outlet in Chicago," Tom says. "I did this for convenience and visibility for my firm."

Then after attending a couple meetings and getting to know some people, Tom joined two key networking organizations: the Chicagoland Chamber of Commerce and the Central Michigan Avenue Association. Both of these organizations provided opportunities to network with businesses that need to get their names in the media.

At the beginning of each month, Tom devises a special networking plan. He looks at three important areas from which to choose his networking activities: what organization events and meetings he can attend, what upcoming meetings and conventions listed in the business press would be worthwhile, and which TV or radio producer or reporter contacts of Andrea's he should arrange to meet that month. He then makes calls, marks dates on his calendar, and follows up.

The meetings he sets up with his media contacts are in addition to ones in which he pitches a particular client or story. Tom simply tries to learn more about his contacts and their publications. This strategy makes it easier to connect when Tom does want to pitch a client or story. Most of the time, these meetings are just for gathering information and staying in touch, but sometimes they lead to bigger opportunities. One time while Tom was having lunch with the editor of a national business publication, the man asked if Tom could recommend someone for a panel on business-to business Internet marketing. Tom introduced him to a contact who was a marketing manager for a national wireless phone company. It was a networking win for Tom for two reasons: First, Tom became a resource for the editor. Second, it gave Tom a reason to reconnect with his contact at the wireless phone company so that he could keep his name in front of him. Subsequently, Tom has had the opportunity to meet with him to discuss future business.

Another part of Tom's networking plan involves day-to-day contacts. He incorporates Andrea's advice to network everywhere, even in the elevator. For example, when Tom is in the elevator on the way up to his office and another person is getting off at a different floor, he sometimes says, "Hi, may I ask what you do on that floor?" So far, he has made connections with a graphics design agency and a national investment firm. "I just keep identifying and expanding my contacts, and my business keeps on growing," he says.

# Organize It All with a Kiss

(**Keep It** Simple, Stupid—Michael's version)

(**Keep It** Simple, Sweetheart—Andrea's version)

Develop a simple system for keeping your contact information readily available. Connecting with just four people a week puts you ahead of most people who claim they're networking. Recall your FOUR-mula for success from Chapter 7, "How to Expand Your Network." Every week, call, email, IM, or write a note to four people:

1. A client, customer, or prospect (remember, we're all in some kind of selling)

2. A former colleague or coworker

3. A former classmate or friend

4. A current classmate or friend

It's so simple!

# Melissa's Story

When Michael introduced Melissa to the idea of networking, she thought it had something to do with computer gadgets. Instead, she found that it meant social networking—or, better yet, professional networking and building contacts to help people change their lives.

She still recalls first hearing about networking: "We were being introduced in class to this idea that we could impact our job hunt, career development, and personal lives by developing a network of people who would be willing to help us if we were willing to help them. We were taught in class to build our personal networks with people we already knew and then continue building it with people we would meet along the way."

As you've learned, networking involves communicating with people on a mutually agreeable time schedule and finding ways to help each other. The simplest and quickest way Melissa built up her network was by joining the online social network sites LinkedIn and Facebook. She created a profile for herself that included information about her education, past and present professions, and interests, among other topics. These memberships allowed her to connect to more people from school and work, as well as people who shared the same interests and goals in life. For contacts Melissa couldn't connect with online, she kept a hard-copy address book and set up a computer database of addresses.

Networking has paid off for Melissa. Her first job out of college was in the medical education field. She got the initial interview through her friendship with a college staffer, who was a friend of the hiring manager of the company. He offered her a job on the spot. Melissa held that position for two years and, during that time, met many highly regarded individuals who became speakers for the company. She developed a large network from this and helped a number of these individuals manage career moves and secure high-level speaking opportunities. As a result, many people in her network have returned or sought to return favors to her.

Melissa has been contacted for a number of positions without ever having to apply. She's even been invited to appear in commercials and work as an extra in a movie, and well-known speaker bureaus call her for help in filling open speaking slots. These are just a few of the benefits she has gotten back from her willingness to help others.

Understandably, she says, "Networking, in my eyes, is a big key to succeeding in almost anything in life."

## It's a Forever Process, and It Isn't Easy

We've all had this experience: Former seminar participants, students, friends, family members, business associates, and even colleagues have approached us and said, "I tried networking once for about three or four months, but I stopped because nothing happened. I didn't get the job I wanted and didn't meet who I wanted. It was too hard, and it didn't work for the amount of effort it took." To these people, we say, "What did you expect to happen in three or four months?" Networking is about building relationships, which takes a lot of time and a lot of work. There's no timetable, no schedule for success. There are no quick and easy formulas, no shortcuts. Networking is hard work. The people who are dedicated to the techniques will be successful; those who aren't dedicated won't be. It's that simple.

## Kristine's Story

College students often doubt the power of networking. They grow up listening to that old tried-and-true statement, "It's not what you know, it's who you know," but nothing brings home the truth of it like graduation day.

Kristine, a student at DeVry University in North Brunswick, New Jersey, learned the importance of networking in college firsthand. "Rolling out of bed, wearing your pajamas to school, and keeping to yourself is no longer an option in college," she says. "That amazing paper you write and leave on your professor's desk could lead you to a desk at the corporate office you have been dreaming about since you signed those acceptance papers. You need to treat every class, every workshop, and every opportunity as a potential connection to your future."

While enrolled in college, Kristine became heavily involved with various activities and clubs on campus, produced A+ work, and showed her professors that she was willing to go above and beyond what was expected. She was polite to every guest on campus, paid attention to the people her mentors and professors knew, and made it a point to obtain employment on campus. As a result of her networking efforts, DeVry faculty voted her valedictorian of both her associate's degree–level class and her bachelor's degree–level class. Kristine also had the opportunity to serve as an officer for many clubs on campus and was nominated as a student representative. Thanks to her on-campus presence, she now has many leads for future employment opportunities.

Kristine discovered that college success revolves around recognizing the importance of networking and taking full advantage of it. There's always someone in a college setting who shares your same interests, is willing to listen to your ideas, or can offer helpful information. Additionally, even if an individual can't help you directly, he or she often can connect you to someone who can, thus proving the importance of networking.

# Summary

Now is the time to choose—it's decision time. As we said early in this book, nearly everyone has the opportunity to choose the pathway to either future success or mediocrity.

Many people will never be aware that they have this opportunity and, therefore, will never choose. The fortunate ones become aware of this opportunity and choose success; others are aware but don't put forth the lifelong effort. The decision pathways are fundamentally a crossroads.

One pathway involves following along and basically handing over your future to whatever you believe life has to offer you. That can be whatever life hands you, whether it is fate, cosmic forces, flock mentality, randomness, luck, predestination, good decisions, or a combination of these and other things that are mostly out of your control.

The other pathway involves choosing networking as a life-altering technique and tool, and then beginning—and never stopping—to use the techniques and tools to choose your life options. Will you still face obstacles, setbacks, job losses, failure, heartbreak, defeat, uncertainty, roadblocks, randomness, and bad luck? Possibly. Many of us do. But you can manage your setbacks, and they should have a less detrimental impact on your life because you'll have the safety net of your network. We cannot predict the future, but if you encounter any or all of these difficulties, you will have techniques and tools to help you face them and realign yourself toward your new goals and objectives. Furthermore, you'll be able to use your network of contacts to help you achieve more, learn more, do more, and be more than you could otherwise.

Many people will want to decide to make networking part of their lives; fewer will actually start, and more will drop away because of the hard work required. However, the dedicated ones (the wolves) will continue on, and they will more likely be successful in achieving their goals and objectives in life. At the end of the race, the others will be on the outside looking in, wondering why they didn't get better jobs, better promotions, or plum assignments; wondering why they didn't get to meet interesting people and do more interesting things; and wondering why they got less out of life than they expected and wanted.

Those on the inside looking out will know the answer: It was in their hands.

---

# 12

# Social Media: Focus on Strategy to Support Your Personal Networking

*By Dr. Michael Lawrence Faulkner*

S ocial media is a phenomenon in which private interactive communication and mass collaboration techniques successfully combine, allowing individuals bound by a shared interest or purpose to transparently and collaboratively connect. If you think this sounds a lot like what many people already refer to as "personal networking," you're correct. Long before social media, the Internet, wireless communications, instant messaging, email, and even the telephone, successful people understood the power of social reciprocity, or the building and maintenance of one's personal contacts for the benefit of both parties.

Social media is the online environment created for the purpose of instant interactive communication and mass collaboration. It is the old campfire, the nineteenth-century family dinner table, the weekly fraternal organization meeting, the PTA, the Sunday afternoon church social, the neighbors gathering at the back fence, and the social networking discussed in this book all rolled into one and magnified by some exponentially large number.

What makes social media different from anything man has done up to this point is the fundamental change in the form of human communications. We can now instantly communicate to one other person or millions of people in seconds through a variety of media using words, pictures, graphics, or code.

Literally any way digital content can be communicated from one person to other people is within our abilities. In this context, social media is about communities of individuals who have come together, joined by a variety of digital communications channels (such as Facebook, Pinterest, YouTube, wireless devices, LinkedIn, Twitter, Digg, Meet-Up, Google Plus, and personal blogs) and bound by a shared interest or purpose. This is what makes social media different from anything man has done up to this point.

The value of social media to support personal networking is found in the productive collaboration of multiple communities, on a massive scale, simultaneously and productively leveraging the knowledge, experience, background, thought leadership, intuition, research, and ideas of many people on a variety of issues, problems, opportunities, and solutions. The benefits of the diversity of heterogeneous thinking (the wisdom of the crowd) all add up to the value of a vast network expanding the value chain of individuals.

## The Functioning of the Parts Is Determined by the Nature of Social Media

The gestalt or behavior of social media is determined by the purposeful configuration and functioning of the individual elements (1) strategy, (2) technology, and (3) audience. These three components are unified as a whole entity; social media cannot achieve its complete purpose simply by attempting to make the parts operate independently.

Social media is a phenomenon in which private interactive communication and mass collaboration techniques successfully combine. It is a set of digital and electronic communications software and various digital technologies that allow individuals to transparently and collaboratively connect, vote, decide, share, judge, evaluate, see, talk, and network with each other. Technologies such as *wikis, social networking, blogs, video posting, peer-to-peer sharing, hashtags, email, instant messaging, cloud storage, bookmarking, share this, threaded discussions, idea engines, answer marketplaces, prediction markets, virtual second worlds, and avatars* are among the current usable and acceptable technologies.

These are the current communication tools and channels. They're not critical, per se—they're parts of the whole phenomena of social media and have a use, but without the strategic purpose or mission of interactive communications and mass collaboration, they're just individual technological game pieces.

By the nature of their demographic and psychographic characteristics, the audiences for social media seek to organize and apply the technologies and parts of social media into a gestalt phenomenon. This phenomenon reconnects individuals and rejects the previous sociological trends of our culture toward atomism and the collapse of community that Robert Putnam described in his 2000 classic study *Blowing Alone.*

Social media can provide far-reaching benefits for two major audiences: individuals and organizations. The first group, individuals, is the only audience we address in this book. Individuals have the potential to use social media to dramatically expand into communities of interest and participate at any level, from being an observer to being an influencer or thought leader of such groups. In addition, individuals can use social media and collaborate primarily by communicating with friends and associates, and they can communicate secondarily to self-brand and self-market.

The Millennial Generation, which makes up 30 percent of the world's population, is driving the social media revolution. In the United States, this generation numbers 81 million, born between 1977 and 1997 during what the author Don Tapscot calls the first net generation. This cohort has changed the rules of communication for the rest of us.

To the fastest-growing influential segment of the population, there is no difference between business and personal communications, no significant difference between public and private communications, and no difference between communicating between two people or among two million people. Communication is a transparent collaboration between those with a common or shared interest.

Regardless of how progressive and enticing this may seem, a caution is in order: Social media is seductive, and it is tempting to try out all the new social media gimmicks, tactics, ideas, concepts, and technology just because they are available and everybody thinks they're cool and hip. There has to be a better reason to become social media literate. One aspect of social media that needs to be reinforced by awareness and skill training is the proven success of strategically applying it to personal networking and job hunting. A great deal of research has clearly demonstrated the benefits of personal networking (referred to previously in this book as the *informal* job hunting approach) as the most effective tool for job searching and career advancement available to individuals.

Another temptation is to repeat the Internet error—to use the vast potential of the medium to oversell and then underperform—by trying to overwhelm as many people as possible with technological cleverness and cuteness, littering the space with spam, junk offers, and other clutter.

The social media train has supposedly left the station, and individuals might feel technologically backward if they haven't kept up. They might feel handicapped if they don't have hundreds of Facebook friends, a Twitter site, or several Google+ circles. This type of thinking is like the "ready, aim, shoot" mentality of the early days of Internet marketing and needs to be rejected. We should already have learned the lessons of the dot.com mistakes, but sometimes it helps to be reminded of what went wrong with the killer app of the World Wide Web.

Peter Drucker, one of the great business thought leaders of the twentieth century and the author of the very first book on the profession of management in 1954, proposed three classic questions about strategic thinking:

1. What is your business?

2. What will be your business?

3. What should be your business?

The questions were seductively subtle, and often individuals (including senior executives) were put off guard by their steamily simplistic substance and missed the important issue Drucker was trying to get them to see. For any individual or firm thinking about employing social media effectively, rethinking and paraphrasing Drucker's three questions is wise.

1. What is your social media strategy?

2. What will be your social media strategy?

3. What should be your social media strategy?

It might seem like a blinding flash of the obvious, but you must approach the job search as you would a full-time job. Dress and think and act like you are being paid to do this.

Approaching the job search or a career enhancement as a full-time job means writing a strategic personal business plan with seven components:

1. Mission statement

2. Vision statement

3. Background and situation analysis

4. Strategic objectives and tactics, including branding and positioning of yourself

5. Targeted potential opportunities, including industry and skill analysis and assessment

6. Reassessment of job skills and current and future needs

7. Social media literacy

As we consider the strategy of social media to support the job search or career enhancement, one very critical point must be front and center: An enormous amount of data demonstrates that employers are looking for *good people* who can adapt and meet the ever-changing needs of business. Employers want skills and characteristics that, for the most part, are transferable to everyone from recent graduates to military veterans.

# What Do Employers Want?

The American Society for Training and Development (ASTD), with the assistance of the U.S. Department of Labor, surveyed Fortune 500 firms in 2011 to determine what skills employers want. The responses in Table 12.1 are displayed in the order of importance to employers.

**Table 12.1**  The Skills Most Desired by Job Applicants for Fortune 500 Firms

| |
|---|
| 1. Teamwork |
| 2. Problem-solving Skills |
| 3. Interpersonal Skills |

| |
|---|
| 4. Oral Communication Skills |
| 5. Listening Skills |
| 6. Creative Thinking |
| 7. Leadership Skills |
| 8. Writing Skills |
| 9. Computation Skills |
| 10. Reading Skills |

In another major study in 2011, called the *Workforce Skills Reality Check,* conducted by the Washington, D.C., consulting firm FTI for the Association of Private Sector Colleges and Universities, more than 1,000 respondents (hiring managers) indicated what they wanted in job applicants. The following list reveals their preferences in job candidates:

- Communication skills
- Honesty and integrity
- Ability to work on diverse teams
- Computer literacy
- Related experience and knowledge
- Reliability, dependability, and responsibility
- Positive attitude and approachable personality
- Ability to continue learning
- Good work ethic, punctuality

Scores of other studies produce similar results. Employers want good people with soft skills—communication skills, integrity, competence, and the ability and experience to find and fix problems.

What is intriguing about the most recent study is that 41 percent of the hiring managers indicated that they were looking to hire, and 85 percent said they were likely to hire soon. However, more than half (54 percent) said it was difficult to find good candidates, and a third (30 percent) indicated that the process of finding good people is getting harder. One of the reasons it's getting harder is that the needs of employers continue to change.

An organization called the Institute for the Future recently identified eight new skills that are relevant and necessary for the twenty-first century:

1. Ability to see the deeper meaning or significance of what is being expressed

2. Novel and adaptive thinking, or proficiency at thinking and coming up with solutions and responses beyond rules or routine

3. Cross-cultural competence, or the ability to operate in different cultural settings

4. Computational thinking, or the ability to translate vast amounts of data into abstract concepts and to understand data-based reasoning

5. Transdisciplinarity, or literacy in and the ability to understand concepts across multiple disciplines

6. Design mindset, or the ability to represent and develop tasks and work processes for desired outcomes

7. Virtual collaboration, or the ability to work productively, drive engagement, and demonstrate presence as a member of a virtual team

8. New media literacy, or the ability to critically assess and develop content that uses new media forms and to leverage these media for persuasive communications

Job seekers must be adroit at demonstrating their ability to translate their personal skills, abilities, characteristics, and background experiences into the skills that employers need now and in the future.

A significant amount of research and writing has been done in this area, and I am currently involved in conducting another major survey on how the supply side (the employers) view, perceive, and use networking. The early results of this research are confirming the data from dozens of previous studies: employers want and need "good people" but generally have trouble finding them.

To me, this says that the formal methods of job search (including digital postings, job fairs, resumes posted on employer websites, recruiters, classified ads, cattle calls, mass mailings of resumes, cover letters, and even what we teach in our educational system) are not working very well.

The literature demonstrates this. As the data indicates, there is more likelihood of a successful job search if job candidates use the informal methods of personal networking and direct application to the hiring manager as major tools. Of course, this is not to say that candidates should not use other tools—they should do so as part of the job search repertory, depending on each candidate and job search.

I previously mentioned the gestalt of social media. It really has three components:

1. The technology
2. The audience
3. The strategic purpose and the audience

This last part is the most important to you. Hundreds of technological tools exist, and they will come and go. Don't get too wrapped up in the individual pieces of the social media technology—they are only the bridge from your strategy to the audience you want to reach.

The audience is your goal, or those you want to reach. Just because the technology can connect you with thousands or even millions of people doesn't mean you need or want to connect. National syndicated columnist and author Peggy Noonan wrote something very profound recently, referring to the ability of the President to reach millions of people by social media. Her comment was that he had a big microphone but no real message.

Integrating social media into your job search requires carefully thinking out the strategy. How do you want social media to support your job search?

Just a decade ago, there was no social media as we think of it today; therefore, there was no need for a social media strategy, per se. However, every individual has a responsibility to spend time daily on visionary and strategic thinking, in addition to focusing on actual tactics and implementing the items of the social media menu.

Social media, like any other phenomena, does not operate in a vacuum. Individuals seeking the advantage of personal networking need to think and plan how social media and their goals will be affected as the social, economic, cultural, and business environment changes.

Virtually no one could have predicted the advent and extraordinary growth of social media (a risk phenomenon we call a "black swan"), but there were early adapters. These individuals recognized the potential value of the possibilities of social media and then the software, technology, media, and tools of social media. The adaptors began as early as possible to explore the individual growth and networking possibilities of social media, and they established practices, benchmarks, and disciplined personal networking management processes of the new media. They gained a huge first-mover type advantage. They became the disciples, teachers, and digital natives.

Some individuals learned valuable lessons from the dot.com boom and bust about maintaining disciplined strategic plans in the midst of speculative run-away technology and individual expectations. The gang speculations of the twenty-somethings who found the Internet saw their technology to be a hallucination or a toy and had no idea what a real strategic plan was, how to target an audience for networking, or how to build an interactive online relationship.

Research data show that the Internet is clearly a channel that the business market is using, but the business advertising dollars do not flow to that channel in proportion to its apparent potential. Data shows that adults are spending 29 percent of their time on the web, but advertisers are putting only 8 percent of their ad spending on the web. Meanwhile, newspapers get only 8 percent of our attention but 20 percent of the ad dollars.

The following examples demonstrate this thinking of individuals and consumers by their behavior.

- According to the FTC, as of 2011, more than 200,000,000 individuals have their names on various federal and state "do not call" lists.

- As of 2011, tens of thousands of consumers have their names on "do not mail" lists.

- Forty-four percent of direct mail advertising is never opened.

- By 2011, tens of thousands of consumers and businesses had their names and businesses on "do not fax" lists.

- As a result of mismanagement, corruption, fraud, misuse, abuse, and the failure of firms to oversee commercial email, the 2003 Federal CAN-SPAN email law was passed. Once the killer application of the Internet, email marketing went from the goose that laid the golden egg to the proverbial dead duck. Commercial email response rates that were as high as 60 percent in the 1990s are now typically in the range of 1 percent to 3 percent—and that's for current customers.

- The Direct Marketing Association (DMA) gives its annual ECHO Award to the top direct response marketing campaigns of the year. Since 1980, the winning direct mail campaigns have displayed consumer response rates of between 1.5 percent and 4 percent.

- Business and commercial trade show attendance has declined 38 percent in the last ten years, but the cost to attend has risen 50 percent.

- Newspaper advertising revenue fell more than 28 percent in one quarter in 2008, and no fewer than 20 U.S. metropolitan newspapers have either gone out of business or gone to a hybrid or online model since 2007.[1]

- People are increasingly turning to the Internet to find information, even local information. Some figures suggest that the use of online search can be as high as 80 percent of all information searches. Dr. Lynella Grant, the author of *Yellow Page Smarts,* makes the point that relying on just the Yellow Pages is no longer safe: More than half of all customers go to the Internet first to find information, even for local products.[2]

- Generator Research predicts that television advertising will fall by more than 75 percent in the next decade.[3]

- Starting in 2007, radio advertising declined 14 consecutive quarters.[4]

- According to an industry expert, as much as 33 percent of all traditional advertising dollars not only are wasted, unproductive, and inefficient, but they cannot even be accounted for.

- Only 18 percent of traditional TV advertising campaigns generate a positive Return on Investment (ROI).[5]

- Only 14 percent of consumers trust advertisements, whereas 79 percent trust peer recommendations.[6]

Over the years, consumers have demonstrated with their buying behavior that traditional forms of marketing, advertising, promotion, branding, sales, and even communications have low levels of effectiveness. Now, since social media has appeared, a new form of communication centers on communities of similarly minded people abundant with passion, experience, thoughts, talents, ideas, solutions, and a desire to collaborate to improve their common interests. This is fertile ground for personal networking.

# The Social Media Channels and the Impact on Personal Networking, Business, and Culture

Among the most prominent news websites geared toward African Americans, many are owned by large media corporations:

- The Grio, an NBC-owned website that was launched in 2009 as a video-focused news site, hired *Tom Joyner Morning Show* commentator Jeff Johnson as a contributor in late 2010. The site received 671,000 unique visitors in November 2010.

- *Washington Post*–owned TheRoot.com was founded by Harvard professor Henry Louis Gates Jr. as a site for commentary on the day's news "from a variety of black perspectives." In November 2010, it had 545,000 unique visitors.

- Radio One's NewsOne, another news site geared toward African Americans, had 359,000 unique visitors in November 2010.

- In January 2011, Huffington Post and BET cofounder Sheila Johnson announced the launch of a section of the Huffington Post devoted to African Americans, called HuffPost GlobalBlack. It is expected to debut in March 2011.

A number of social media websites target African Americans. The most popular include these:

- **Black Planet.com:** www.blackplanet.com. Initially, BlackPlanet was designed as a way for African-American professionals to network. Since then, it has grown and evolved as a site operating under the principles of Web 2.0. Members can read other members' blogs, watch music videos, chat with one another, look for new careers, and discuss news. Although BlackPlanet is not restricted to any community, this site is more popular among African Americans. It helped Obama connect to nearly 200,000 potential supporters.

- **BlackBusinessWomenOnLine:** www.mybbwo.com. This is a social network for black businesswomen and women entrepreneurs.

- **Black Business Space:** www.blackbusinessspace.com. Black Business Space is a community of business owners, entrepreneurs, professionals, and consumers who want to build beneficial relationships.

- **BlackBloggersConnect.com:** A social network connecting African American bloggers, this website is also a resource guide for African American bloggers, writers, and journalists.

- **SeeingGrowth.com:** Promotes self and community growth through the collaboration of talents and thoughts.

- **BlackFathers.org:** A site celebrating generations of strong and loving African American fathers.

- **BlackBloggersNetwork.com:** A social network and resource for African American bloggers, writers, and journalists.

- **BloggingWhileBrown.com:** Promotes conferences on African American issues and speakers

- **DelawareBlack.com:** Provides digital news of the African American community in the Delaware area.

The trade associations and professional societies that represent just about every industry, line of business, profession, and interest group are excellent places to build your personal networking.

Next are the top 21 oldest and largest national black professional groups, as compiled by Dan Woog, Monster Contributing Writer.

## *Business*

- **BDPA:** www.bdpa.org. Organized in 1975. The BDPA has more than 40 chapters. The organization is open to African Americans in data processing and related fields.

- **National Association of Black Accountants** (NABA): www.nabainc.org. Founded in 1969. The goal of the NABA is to represent the more than 200,000 African-American professionals in accounting and finance.

- **National Association of African Americans in Human Resources (NAAAHR):** www.naaahr.org. The NAAAHR is a national organization of human resource professionals, with 36 local chapters. It includes consultants and students.

- **National Black Business Trade Association (NBBTA):** www.nbbta.org. The NBBTA is a self-help resource and networking group founded in 1993 that provides businesspeople with information, products, services, and technologies.

- **National Black MBA Association (NBMBAA):** www.nbmbaa.org. The NBMBAA is an 8,000-member professional organization made up of African-American graduates with MBAs and advanced degrees. Established in 1970, its mission is to increase the number and diversity of African Americans in business.

- **National Sales Network (NSA):** www.salesnetwork.org. The NSA is an association of African-American sales and sales management professionals. Organized in 1992, with more than 2,000 members in 16 chapters.

## Design

- **Organization of Black Designers (OBD):** www.obd.org. The OBD consists of 10,000 design professionals in visual communications, as well as graphic, interior, fashion, and industrial design.

## Engineering and Science

- **American Association of African Americans in Energy (AABE):** www.aabe.org. The AABE was founded in 1977; it has 36 chapters. Specialties include energy policy, technology, and the environment.

- **National Organization for the Professional Advancement of Black Chemists and Chemical Engineers (NOBCChE):** www. nobcche.org. This organization was created in 1972 to build a community of minority scientists and engineers; it has 39 professional and university chapters.

- **National Society of Black Engineers (NSBE):** www.nsbe.org. Started in 1975, the NSBE now has more than 35,700 members and more than 390 college, precollege, and technical professional chapters nationwide and overseas. The group's mission is to increase the number of African-American engineers, as well as help them succeed professionally and to give back to their communities.

- **National Society of Black Physicists (NSBP):** www.nsbp.org. NSBP is the largest organization of African-American physicists. It has 16 sections, ranging from astronomy, astrophysics, and nuclear physics to technology transfer, business development, and entrepreneurship. Its mission is to promote the professional well-being of African-American physicists within the international scientific community.

## Food Services

- **BCA:** www.bcaglobal.org. The BCA was incorporated as the Black Culinary Alliance in 1998 and is now known by its acronym. It is a national educational and networking organization that serves African Americans and other minority professionals working in hospitality and food services.

## General

- **100 Black Men of America:** www.100blackmen.org. 100 Black Men of America was founded in 1963 and now has more than 110 chapters and over 10,000 members. Its mission includes leadership, mentoring, education, health, and economic development.

## Government

- **African Americans in Government (BIG):** www.bignet.org. BIG members are civil servants at the federal, state, county, and municipal levels. The organization was founded in 1975. Its more than 50 chapters include the Departments of State and Homeland Security, the Coast Guard, and the National Institutes of Health.

## Healthcare

- **National Black Nurses Association (NBNA):** www.nbna.org. The NBNA was organized in 1971. It has 80 chapters representing more than 150,000 African American nurses in the United States, the Caribbean, and Africa.

- **National Medical Association (NMA):** www.nmanet.org. The NMA is the oldest (founded in 1895) and largest national professional organization for African-American physicians. A leading force for parity in medicine, it provides educational programs and conducts outreach efforts.

- **Student National Medical Association (SNMA):** www.snma.org. The SNMA is the largest organization focused on the needs and concerns of African-American medical students and residents.

### Law and Criminal Justice

- **National Association of African Americans in Criminal Justice (NABCJ):** www.nabcj.org. The NABCJ was organized in 1974, and it has state and local chapters across the United States. Members include law enforcement personnel, corrections officers, court employees, social services workers, academics, and clergy.

- **National Bar Association (NBA):** www.nationalbar.org. The NBA has been an advocate for social justice since 1925; it promotes professional development for African Americans in the legal profession. The organization has more than 20,000 member lawyers, judges, educators, and law students.

- **National Organization of Black Law Enforcement Executives (NOBLE):** www.noblenational.org. Founded in 1976, this public service organization serves as the "conscience of law enforcement."

## Media

- **National Association of Black Journalists (NABJ):** www.nabj.org. NABJ is a professional organization for African Americans working in print, radio, television, new media, and related areas. It was founded in 1975.

In addition, Renee is a member of this organization:

- **National Coalition of 100 Black Women (NCBW):** www.ncbw.org. The NCBW is a national organization that advocates on behalf of black women through national and local alliances that promote its national and international agendas on leadership development and on gender equity in health, education, and economic development.

According to William Jackson's blog[7], African Americans have a growing presence on Facebook, Google+, Nings, YouTube, Blog Talk Radio, and Tweeting While Black.

Entrepreneurialism, such as Tiffany Duhart's eblast (www.nokturnal-escape.com) and Facebook presence (www.facebook.com/nokturnal-escape), has seen great growth because of the information provided on community events.

According to eMarketer.com, based on a year-long survey in 2011 by Experian Simmons, African Americans are more actively engaged in mobile phone use, particularly for social contacts.

# Data on Social Media for the General Population

Social media changes at the speed of light. From our research, we pulled the following facts that give you an idea of how fast these vehicles are growing.

- Facebook has more than a billion users (more than 300,000 are businesses).

- An average 200,000,000 people sign on monthly to Twitter and spend 132 minutes on the site.

- LinkedIn has 100,000,000 monthly visitors.

- Seventy-three percent of the American population uses the Internet regularly, and two thirds (65.8 percent) of adults with an Internet connection use social media in some form.

- Forty-six percent of the global population visits a social networking site daily; one third of these visits (about 30 percent of the global population, or 2.41 billion people) are looking for brands to interact with online.

- A recent Jupiter Research study found that 50 percent of Internet shoppers consulted a social media blog before making the Internet purchase.[8] Furthermore there are more than 115 million active blog sites just in English and perhaps twice that number if foreign language blogs are counted.

- In 2008, the most popular Facebook application was not a game, a peer-to-peer music sharing app, a video, or a TV app. The most popular Facebook application was Causes, which let users start and join causes they cared about. It had nearly 20,000,000 active monthly users.

- By some estimates, the adoption of online voting in the future could save the U.S. economy an estimated $6.7 billion in lost productivity.

- According to a Nielsen 2010 study, U.S. Internet users spend three times more time on blogs and social media networks than email.

- Fifty-seven percent of American workers use social media for business purposes at least once a week.[9]

- The Library of Congress (LOC) has recognized the significance of social media and established the National Digital Information Infrastructure and Preservation Program. According to its website, the LOC is pursuing a strategy of collecting, preserving, and making available significant digital content, especially information that is created in digital format only. This work is being done so that current and future generations will have access to the content. In April 2010, the LOB announced that it would begin archiving all Twitter messages, retroactive to 2006.

The media components of social media (Facebook, Twitter, Google+, YouTube, Foursquare, BrightKite, Groupon, LinkedIn, and others) and software and technological components (blogs, digital video, bookmarking, microblogging, media sharing, aggregators, and so on) function to bring individuals, firms, and organizations together as collaborative communities working to solve problems, fill needs gaps, find solutions to problems, develop collective answers to questions, and provide the wisdom of crowds.

If Peter Drucker were alive today, he might ask, "What is your social media strategy?"

Think about it.

If you're an individual, isn't it to find a better, more efficient, more effective way to find, keep, update, locate, and communicate with friends, associates, family members, and persons of interest in communities of special interest? At its simplest, it is a great opportunity to individually or in collaborative communities do the following:

- Gain more opportunities to build, develop, and improve your personal networking.

- Get more personal branding and exposure for you and your ideas, beliefs, and values.

- Increase online recommendations and referrals.

- Get and give advice.

- Share opinions.

- Demonstrate your expertise.

- Perform or publish your work.

- Acknowledge something or someone.

- Distribute software, content, or art forms (legally).

- Create targeted discussion groups.

- Share photos, music, and content.

- Post and/or get resumes.

- Get answers to questions.

- Play games alone or in combination with others.

- Solve problems (social, academic, political, scientific, geopolitical, engineering, and so on).

- Announce events and activities.

It should be apparent to individuals that social media requires a commitment to transparency, honesty, and open and authentic communications. These are fundamental to the foundation on which personal networking succeeds. The strategy is to select technological tools that help achieve the purpose of networking.

The whole purpose of social media (and the whole purpose of the Internet, but we missed that one) is to create, build, and sustain relationships through communication channels that people prefer. Then, if appropriate, the relationship turns into a long-term personal networking commitment.

Acquaintances will become close long-term friends. If building interpersonal, interactive, sustainable relationships is the goal, then friendships, networking relationships, and long-term commitments will naturally result, if appropriate.

Some people will still say, "The Internet came, and although it had a huge impact, it did not alter traditional business as much as the hype predicted." These people will say that social media is similar—lots of hype, but when the dust settles, we will be back to business as usual. The arguments that social media is mostly hype and will fade away are being addressed by the successes of social media. The debate on the exact impact of the Internet on our culture and business will not be resolved for many years to come. However, one critical factor in play today was not as powerful a factor in the 1990s, and that is the generational demographics.

What force or forces have led us to this critical change at this point in time? The answer can be found in a combination of factors: the changing demographics of our population and the power of technology to produce ever more efficient and less costly tools by which to communicate.

We will see and experience the impact of a growing and younger workforce dominated by people under the age of 30 who view communications, not as boomers do, but as separate experiences. To younger workers, there is no difference between private and business communications because almost all communications are (or should be) through social media channels. The communications thus are cooperative and collaborative in nature.

The population that has rapidly adopted the tools and technology of social media has a dramatically different perspective on communications. To them, communications (private or business) is 24/7. The social media tools, technology, and software have continued to be developed, improved, and deployed at ever more productive rates and efficient costs, helping to blur the lines and alter the paradigm of communications. Work and private lives are blended because human beings are adapting to a form of communication and cooperative leadership that involves more collaboration teaming than the outlook of "Here it is—this is the way it is going to be."

The major factors in the rapid adoption of social media at this time are the growing numbers of digital natives in groups of influence who believe personal communication is not divided into personal and business, and the growing proliferation of free, real-time social media communications platforms.

The digital natives, the Millennial Generation, got it intuitively; hopefully more of us gray beards are coming to realize the benefits as well. To put things in terms we invented, the value is in the "workflow output measurement." Social media reduces inefficient and multiple individual redundancies, but expands the real personal networking function. We show this in actual cases, but it is simply accomplished by many people sharing experiences, reviews, complaints, ideas, and solutions, and the output of these communities being acted with complete transparency.

## Back to the Future

A side benefit of the growth in social media that not many people have spoken about is that all this reconnecting is hopefully rebuilding our social capital. In 2000, author Robert Putnam wrote the bestselling book *Bowling Alone,* in which he reported the results of his long-term study of the loss of social capital in America.

Putnam traced the long, slow decline of group and social communities in America from the end of World War II to the late twentieth century. His research demonstrated the decline in membership organizations of all types, from PTAs to trade associations, bridge clubs to volunteer membership organizations, and unions to bowling leagues. What concerned Putnam along with the decline of membership organizations and groups was the resulting decline in social capital.

As Putnam pointed out, physical capital refers to properties of individuals, and social capital refers to the connections among individuals—social networks and norms of reciprocity and trustworthiness that arise from them.[10] In Putnam's analysis we simply were no longer doing good things for others because of the subsequent decline in personal contacts with one another.

The term *social capital* itself was used by theoreticians, scholars, researchers, and others as early as 1916 to stress the importance of community involvement for successful schools. In the 1950s, Canadian sociologists used the term to characterize the club memberships of well-to-do suburbanites.

In the 1960s, urban specialist Jane Jacobs used the term to laud neighborliness in modern metropolitan areas. In the 1970s, economist Glenn Loury used the term in his theory to analyze the legacy of slavery. In the 1980s, French social theorist Pierre Bourdieu used the term to describe the social and economic resources embodied in social networks. Putnam then brought forth his own insights into how today's social media is connected to social capital, not just in the sense of individual social clout and companionship, but also in terms of how both individuals (private good) and the community (public good) benefit.[11] Now social media could be the catalyst that can reignite an awakening of social capital. It might not be through the face-to-face contacts Putnam had hoped for, but social media certainly encourages individual collaboration, teamwork, mutual obligations, norms of reciprocity, cooperation, and work toward the greater community good.

## The Perils of Predictions

Having positioned social media in this context, it is equally important to provide an abstract of contrary points of view. Some people believe we have already reached a "saturation level" for social media.

When people, even knowledgeable and respected sources such as Forrester, attempt to make predictions about anything that involves "technology," my first thought is to wonder why they want to expose themselves to eventual ridicule (people remember the bloopers, not who was right on target). By their nature, predictions are risky gambits—at best, making predictions is like putting a puzzle together in the dark and without all the pieces, and then trying to describe your finished work in detail.

Social media is a phenomenon resulting more from the changes in the forms of human communication than from insightful business managers looking for a better mouse trap. The principle or phenomenon and the technology are not the same; the technology is built based upon the phenomenon. In practice, before phenomena can be used for technology, they must be harnessed and set up to work; phenomena can rarely work in their raw form, yet today's predictions are being made using current technology.

## Social Media Isn't for Everyone

Not every individual, business, or organization will adapt social media to their lives or business model. Social media is not applicable for some; others are just not ready to accept the benefits and value of social media.

Misuse of social media also can cause high failure rates. Social media is not suitable when deep analysis is required, when intermediaries or experts require information, when certain safeguards or security standards are required, or when sharing with large groups is inappropriate. Regardless, social media is having an extraordinary impact on individuals and businesses and, therefore, should be understood.

A July 2009 Nielsen Study–Global Online Consumer Survey found that only 14 percent of consumers trust advertising, but 78 percent trust peer recommendations from social media. Other benefits are related to the growth of social media with regard to transparency. For individuals, the adoption of social media means we are composing and transmitting content in the form of hundreds or thousands of short messages, full text documents, video clips, and other content destined for far-off places. This then extends our potential networks. The Gartner Group did an extensive study of social media beginning in 2009, and one of the most interesting findings was a striking discovery that most social media initiatives in companies and organizations fail. Either they don't attract any interest or they never create measurable business value.[12]

What is surprising about this is, given the fact that half of most businesses' or organizations' customers, prospects, leads, members, students, donors, associates, contacts, stakeholders, and competition are using social media, most businesses and organizations are only reaching half of their markets on a channel that they have not even seriously considered.

It seems many businesses and organizations either want to try social media but want to keep it tightly corralled within existing marketing processes and operational procedures, or let it do its own thing. Both approaches are wrong. Whether it is based on a business model or is for individual use, social media needs a strategic plan.

# Endnotes

1. www.newspaperdeathwatch.com. Accessed 12 June 2012.

2. Even Wall Street acknowledges that the days of printed directories such as the Yellow Pages are numbered. The *Wall Street Journal* reported that advertising in U.S. print directories is expected to fall 39 percent over the next four years—in their words, *"as people migrate en masse to the web."*

3. Jason Falls and Eric Deckers, *No Bullshit Social Media: The All-Business, No-Hype Guide to Social Media* (Indianapolis, IN: Pearson Education, 2012).

4. Bruce Barton, "Television Advertising: An Irreversible Decline?" *Contacto Magazine,* www.contactomagazine.com/biznews/tvadvertisingslup0309.html.

5. Erik Qualman, *Socialnomics: How Social Media Transforms the Way We Live and Do Business* (Hoboklen, NJ: John Wiley & Sons, 2009).

6. *Ibid.*

7. *Ibid.*

8. http://jacksonville.com/opinion/blog/400553/william-jackson/2011-12-27/african-americans-technology-and-social-media. Accessed 5 May 2012.

9. iCrossing, "How America Searches; Health and Wellness," 14 January 2008, http://newsicrossing.compress_releass..php?press_release=icrossingstudy-finds-internet-top-resource-for-health-information.

10. Robert Putnam, *Bowling Alone* (New York: Simon & Schuster, 2000).

11. *Ibid* (p. 20, 2000).

12. Anthony Bradley and Mark McDonald, *The Social Organization: How to Use Social Media to Tap the Collective Genius of Your Customers and Employees* (Boston: Harvard Business School Publishing, 2011).

# Sources

Faulkner, M. 2009. LinkedIn: "My Polls." http://polls.linkedin.com/. Accessed 30 June 2010.

Forrester NACTAS, Q2. 2006. *Youth, Media, and Marketing and Financial Online Survey.* Cambridge, MA.

Forrester Research. Gray, C. F., and E. W. Larson. 2008. *Project Management: The Management Process, 4th ed.* New York: McGraw-Hill/Irwin.

Gallup. 2009. *Strengths-based Development: Using Strengths to Accelerate Performance.* www.gallup.com/consulting/61/Strengths-Development.aspx. Accessed 10 January 2010.

Hart, P. 2006. *How Should Colleges Prepare Students to Succeed in Today's Global Economy?* Washington, D.C.: Association of American Colleges and Universities.

Nierenberg, A. 2002. *Nonstop Networking.* Sterling, VA: Capital Books.

# Index

## Numbers

2-2-2 strategy, 87
100 Black Men of America, 143

## A

AABE (American Association of
   African Americans in Energy), 142
acquaintances, 43
active listening, 63
activities
   etiquette, 104-105
   identifying those where people you
      want to know gather, 81-86
adopting attitudes and behaviors for
   networking, 19
   first impressions, 19-23
advertising, 137-139
   social media, 151
African Americans in Government
   (BIG), 143
American Association of African
   Americans in Energy (AABE), 142
American Society for Training and
   Development (ASTD), 133
anniversaries, 92
applicants for jobs, what you need to
   do, 15-16
appreciation, 50
articles, writing, 89
attending events, tips for
   introverts, 69-70

attitudes, 115, 116
   giving yourself permission, 25-27
   for networking, 19
      *first impressions, 19-23*
   photographer's story, 116-117
attractiveness, 21
audience, social media, 136
auditory-type people, 48

## B

baby steps, tips for introverts, 66-68
bad habits, listening, 63
BCA (Black Culinary Alliance), 143
BDPA, 141
become a resource for others, 98
become known, 89
behaviors for networking, 19
   first impressions, 19-23
benefits of social media, 147
BIG (African Americans in
   Government), 143
birthdates, 92
Black Business Space, 140
Black Business Women OnLine, 140
Black Culinary Alliance (BCA), 143
Black Planet, 140
BlackBloggersConnect.com, 140
BlackBloggersNetwork.com, 140
BlackFathers.org, 140
BloggingWhileBrown.com, 140
BNI (Business Network
   International), 82
body language, 20-21

# I

icebreakers, 28-31

idea-generator topics, 34-35

identifying

    organizations and activities where people you want to know gather, 81-86

    people who can help you, 78-79, 122

      *Tom's story, 122-123*

IM (instant messaging), etiquette, 107

important dates, 92

industry-specific groups, 83-84

interests, 92

Internet, networking online, 71-74

interpersonal skills, 8

introductions

    branding statements, 31-32

    etiquette, 106-107

    introducing yourself to hosts, 36

    introducing yourself to speakers, 37

introverts, 61

    advantages when networking, 61-62

    listening, 62-63

    online social networking, 71-74

    passion, 65

    techniques for networking, 65

      *attend events, 69-70*

      *compliments, 68*

      *eye contact, 68-69*

      *having objectives, 66*

      *network at your highest energy level time of day, 70-71*

      *one-on-one meetings, 70*

      *recharge and reward yourself, 71*

      *scripts, 68*

      *set time limits, 71*

      *taking baby steps, 66-68*

involvement, expanding your network, 86-89

# J

Jackson, William, 144

Jacobs, Jane, 150

job candidates, characteristics of, 7-8

job search, 135-136

    social media, 133, 136-139

jobs

    finding through networking, 6-8

    how positions are filled, 13-14

    what applicants need to do, 15-16

Johnson, Jeff, 139

Johnson, Sheila, 139

joining

    committees, 88

    groups, 36

# K

keeping in touch

    creating a system for your growing network, 99-100

    email, 96

    face-to-face time, 99

    follow up, 97-98

    gifts, 96-97

    notes, 93

      *congratulations, 94*

      *FYI notes, 94*

      *handwritten notes, 93*

      *holiday notes, 95*

      *nice talking with you notes, 94*

      *Power of Three, 95-96*

      *thank you notes, 93-94*

      *thinking of you notes, 94*

keeping score, 111

    etiquette, 110-111

Kennedy, Randall, 22

kinesthetic, 49

KISS (Keep It Simple, Stupid), 113, 124

    Melissa's story, 124-125

know who you are, 117

Kristine's story, 126-127